Catherine of Siena

Doctor of the Church

Notes on Her Life and Teaching

Giacinto D'Urso, OP

Translated with Introduction and Notes
by Thomas McDermott, OP

NEW PRIORY PRESS

EXPLORING THE DOMINICAN VISION

2013

Translation of Giacinto D'Urso, OP, "Santa Caterina da Siena" in
Temi di predicazione XIV/84 (1970): pp. 13 -126. With permission
of the Editorial Director.

CONTENTS

INTRODUCTION

The year 2010 marks the fortieth anniversary of Pope Paul VI's proclamation of St. Catherine of Siena (1347-1380) a Doctor of the Church and yet her doctrine or teaching is largely unknown to theologians and students of spirituality. This is owing to several factors: her major work, the *Dialogue*, was dictated in a mystical state and over a period of time and, therefore, contains interruptions, repetitions, and overlapping arguments; her spiritual thought relies mostly on images instead of definitions; it is necessary to read not only the *Dialogue* but also her 381 letters, which are actually more like spiritual conferences, and twenty-six prayers in order to have a comprehensive understanding of her thought. And for those of us who live in the English-speaking world, the Cather-inian corpus was not translated in its entirety until 2009.

As a result of these factors, very little has been written about Catherine's teaching and often that which has is flawed because writers do not have a grasp of her whole teaching. Such writings are often brief thematic studies on such topics as her understanding of the Eucharist, the Cross, the Blood, social justice, etc. It's not surprising that some students of spirituality have come to the unfortunate conclusion that Catherine's spiritual thought is confused and even contradictory. The frustration can be heard in the words of one Jesuit commentator some years ago: "More problems than he deserves stand in the way of the student who would learn of St. Catherine, the mystic."[i] But the truth of the matter was expressed by Paul VI in his apostolic letter *Mirabilis in ecclesia Deus* (1971) when he refers to the "definite coherence of her teachings" and how "the various sections of Catherine's teaching form a closely-knit, compact whole."[ii]

Giacinto D'Urso, OP

Giacinto (Hyacinth) D'Urso (1913-2002), Dominican friar of the Province of San Marco and Sardegna (later the Roman Province), is regarded by many Italian commentators as the foremost expert on the mysticism of Catherine of Siena. After his ordination in 1936 he obtained a doctorate in theology from the Angelicum in Rome. He served the Order in various capacities as novice master, prior, pastor, preacher and, for a time, professor of theology at the Angelicum. For many years he was the editor of the acclaimed Dominican spirituality journal *Rivista di ascetica e mistica* and was a lifelong student of the spirituality of Fra Angelico, St. Antoninus, Blessed Angela of Foligno, but in a particular way of the thought of St. Catherine of Siena of whom he was a devoted *Caterinato*.

The *Bibliografia analitica di S. Caterina da Siena* 1901-2000 lists 107 scholarly articles written by Fr. D'Urso between 1940 and 2000. Some of the more important ones were collected and published by the National Center of Catherinian Studies in Rome under the title *Il genio di Santa Caterina* (1971). He and Alvaro Grion, OP, were the major theological contributors to the official *positio* commissioned by the Vatican in preparation for Catherine being proclaimed Doctor. It was not the last time that Fr. D'Urso's expertise was to be put at the service of the universal Church as the echo of his voice can be heard in the apostolic letter of Paul VI mentioned above as well as in John Paul II's apostolic letter *Amantissima providentia* (1980) for the sixth centenary of Catherine's death.

The Present Work

In 1970, the year Catherine was proclaimed Doctor, Fr. D'Urso wrote his *magnum opus*, a 113-page article, in the form of notes, on the life and teaching of the Sienese saint in the review *Temi di predicazione* published by the Dominicans in Naples. It was only in this article, a translation of which is the book you are now holding, that he ever attempted a comprehensive exposition of her teaching. D'Urso brought to this work a classical theological training, knowledge of mysticism in general, his Dominican vocation, and an ardent love of Catherine. He is careful and thorough in his summaries and analyses; his conclusions are balanced and reliable. His style is literary, succinct, and dense. Most important, his scholarship reveals new depths to Catherine's thought, making for a new appreciation of her on the 40th anniversary of Paul VI's proclamation.

Plan of the Work

D'Urso's profound comprehension of Catherine's doctrine is first seen in the structure of the work itself which is a fruit of his thoughtful analysis. After presenting some notes on Catherine's life, he turns his attention to her teaching. First, he considers the theme of knowledge: knowledge of self and knowledge of God in self which result in awareness of our spiritual poverty and awaken in us a desire to grow in knowledge and love of God, union with whom is our final end. He then presents Catherine's two principal teachings on spiritual growth: the "tree of charity" and the "bridge of Christ crucified." The former pertains essentially to growth in the virtues; the more we are conformed to the virtuous humanity of Christ, the more we are filled with his deifying Spirit.

The Christ-Bridge is Catherine's mature and more comprehensive image of the entire spiritual journey. Here, the pilgrim soul is attracted by the sensation of love coming from the head of the cross (Catherine's interpretation of Christ's words in Jn 12:32, "And I, when I am lifted up from the earth, will draw all people to myself") and, as one responds to this invitation, his or her knowledge and love of God gradually increase while passing through three and, ultimately, four progressive stages of growth before becoming the "son" or child of God at which point one arrives at the gate at the end of the bridge and at the brink of the "abyss of love" which is the Trinity.

D'Urso would be the first to admit that Catherine's teaching cannot be systematized. His scholarship reveals, nonetheless, its inner coherence and lack of contradiction. It is as if D'Urso turns over an old log on the forest floor to reveal a plethora of life underneath; such is the richness of her teaching which, far from being difficult to understand, is quite easy.

Catherine did not belong to the cloister but lived in the world throughout her life; her teaching is an expression of her Dominican vocation of preaching for the "salvation of souls." It is directed to Christians in all walks of life and is eminently practical in its application to the day-to-day lives of believers. John Paul II aptly called her teaching a "lived theology."[iii] Its distinctiveness, compared to the writings of other mystics, is noted by Benedict Ashley, OP:

> To me, Catherine's spiritual teaching is more relevant for our times and closer to the heart of the gospel than that of many other mystics, even some of the greatest. She is little concerned with imaginative meditations on the Lord's life, like Bridget of Sweden or Henry Suso; nor with metaphysical speculation, like Meister Eckhart; nor with the psychological phases of dark nights and inner illumi-nations, like Ruysbroeck, Teresa of Avila, and John of the Cross. Although her life is filled with extraordinary experiences and crises both within and without, yet none of this is

central to her spirituality. What concerns her is to gaze with the "eye of faith" into the clear light of the gospel and, by this light, to work ceaselessly for the renewal of the Church, of the world, and of those dear friends who have need of her.[iv]

Acknowledgements

I wish to thank Daniele Cara, OP, Provincial of the Roman Province of the Order of Preachers, and Giuseppe Piccinno, OP, Editorial Director of *Temi di Predicazione* in which this work first appeared, for their gracious permission to publish this translation. I also wish to thank Sister M. Imelda Fortuna, OP, of the Dominican Sisters of St. Catherine of Siena of Montemario, Rome, for her invaluable assistance. It is my hope that this work will help to make Catherine of Siena's magnificent doctrine more widely known and studied.

Thomas McDermott, OP
Regent of Studies
Province of St. Albert the Great, USA
1909 South Ashland Avenue
Chicago, IL 60608

viii

Chronology^v

1347 On March 25, the feast of the Annunciation, Catherine is born at Siena with her twin sister Giovanna, the twenty-third and twenty-fourth children of the cloth-dyer Jacopo di Benincasa and his wife Lapa di Puccio Piagenti.

1353 Catherine's experiences her first vision, "the vision of the royal Christ," while walking down the via del Costone near her home.

1354 Catherine makes a vow of virginity.

1362 Her favorite sister, Buonaventura, dies. Shortly thereafter Catherine cuts off her hair to forestall her parent's plans to marry her off. Fra' Tommaso dalla Fonte, OP, a cousin who grew up in her home, becomes her confessor.

1363 (c.) Catherine declares publicly that she has no intention of ever marrying. She begins fasting. She is clothed in the habit of the *Mantellate* or Dominican sisters of penance and begins living in seclusion in a "cell" or small room in the family house for three years.

1367 (c.) She experiences the mystical espousals with Christ and then receives the mission of working in the world in his name for the salvation of her neighbor. She gradually leaves her cell and performs corporal works of mercy. She is granted a vision of the soul's beauty. A "family" of spiritual disciples begins to gather around her.

1368 A year of great political turbulence and upheavals. On August 22 Catherine's father dies. Around this time Fra' Bartolomeo Dominici, OP, joins her circle of disciples and eventually becomes her second confessor.

1370 The summer was one of great mystical experiences for Catherine: the mystical exchange of hearts with the Lord, mystical death, and other wonderful gifts.

1372 Catherine writes her first political letters for the sake of peace in Italy. Her fasting is now almost total.

1373   With the support of the pope, Catherine promotes the idea of a crusade.

1374   She goes to Florence at the time of the general chapter of the Dominicans. Fra' Raymond of Capua is assigned as her confessor, and becomes her friend and biographer. Catherine re-enters Siena where the plague has again struck; she nurses the plague-stricken and cures Raymond and Matteo di Centi. The plague ends and she goes to Montepulciano for the first time.

1375   Journey to Pisa, where on April 1 she receives the invisible stigmata in the chapel of Santa Cristina. Returning to Siena, she converts and assists Niccolò di Toldo, a prisoner condemned to death. Florence revolts against the pope and war begins.

1376   On March 31 Florence is put under papal interdict. Catherine, at the request of the Florentines, goes to Avignon to intercede for them and to encourage the pope to return to Rome. Gregory XI leaves Avignon on September 13. Catherine passes through Tolone, frees Varazze of the plague, and encourages Gregory at Genova. She returns to Siena in December.

1377   On January 17 Gregory XI enters Rome. Catherine writes to him and pleads on behalf of Siena which has now joined with Florence in the antipapal rebellion. In the summer she sets forth on an extended mission of peace and reconciliation among the noble families in the Val d'Orcia, after having begun work to transform the castle at Belcaro, close to Siena, into a monastery for cloistered nuns. In late summer she sends Raymond of Capua to Rome with certain proposals for the reform of the church. After an intense mystical experience, Catherine begins dictating the *Dialogue* sometime around October. On December 13 she is sent by the pope to Florence to sue for peace.

1378   On March 27 Gregory XI dies and Urban VI is elected on April 8. On June 18 Catherine is nearly killed by a mob in Florence during the revolt of the Ciompi and she retires for a little while outside the city. Peace between Florence and the pope is reached on July 28. She again goes to Siena and finishes dictating the *Dialogue*. On September 20 the antipope Clement VII is elected at Fondi resulting in schism. Catherine is called to Rome by Urban VI, leaves Siena with the *"bella brigata,"* her band of approximately forty disciples, and arrives at the Eternal City on November 28. She is immediately received by the pope and speaks before the cardinals. In December at the port of Ostia she says farewell for the last time to Raymond of Capua who has been sent by the pope on a mission to France pertaining to the schism.

1379   During the year Catherine sends letters and messengers from Rome to every part of the Christian world in support of the cause of the true pope. She calms the Romans who revolt against the pope and blesses Tommaso d'Alviano who defeats the antipapal troops at Marino resulting in the recovery of Castel San Angelo in Rome. Most of her prayers were recorded during this time.

1380   Amid terrible physical and moral trials, Catherine's physical condition worsens day-by-day. With difficulty she walks every day to St. Peter's basilica where she spends the day praying for the church. On January 29–30 she has her final great mystical experience in which she offers her life for the church. She dies in Rome during the morning of April 29. She is buried at the church of Santa Maria sopra Minerva in Rome; her head is later transferred to the church of San Domenico in Siena.

1461   On June 29 Catherine is canonized by Sienese Pope Pio II (Piccolomini).

1970   On October 4 Paul VI includes Catherine in the catalogue of doctors of the universal church together with St. Theresa of Avila. They are the first women saints to be declared doctors.

[i] Elmer O'Brien, SJ, *Varieties of Mystic Experience* (New York: New American Library, 1964), p. 147.

[ii] Paul VI, Apostolic Letter, *Mirabilis in Ecclesia Deus. Acta Apostolicae Sedis* 63:9 (September 30, 1971), §3, p. 679.

[iii] John Paul II, Apostolic Letter, *Novo millennio ineunte*, §27 (2001), at www.vatican.va.

[iv] Benedict Ashley, OP, "Guide to Saint Catherine's Dialogue," *Cross and Crown* 29 (September 1977), p. 248.

[v] This is in large part a translation, with some modifications, of Giacinto D'Urso's "Nota Biografica," in Santa Caterina da Siena, *L'estasi e la parola*: *Dialogo della divina provvidenza, lettere, orazioni*. Testi scelti a cura di Giacinto D'Urso (Fiesole: Nardini Editore, 1996), pp. 43–45. I have also consulted: Kenelm Foster, "Key Events in Catherine's Life," in *I, Catherine: Selected writings of Catherine of Siena*. Ed. and trans. Kenelm Foster, OP, and Mary John Ronayne, OP. (London: Collins, 1980), pp. 49–50; Suzanne Noffke, OP, "Chronology of Catherine's Life," in Catherine of Siena, *The Letters of Catherine of Siena*. Trans. Suzanne Noffke, OP. (Tempe, Arizona: Arizona Center for Medieval and Renaissance Studies, 2000), Vol. I, pp. liii-lvi.

CHAPTER ONE

LIFE AND WORKS OF ST. CATHERINE

Catherine's Life

Childhood and Vocation: Hidden Life

Catherine was born in Siena in 1347, the twenty-fourth child of the cloth dyer Jacopo di Benincasa and Mona Lapa Piagenti in the quarter of the city known as Fontebranda.[1] At the age of six she had her first vision; at seven she made a vow of virginity to the Lord in the hands of the Blessed Virgin. Having knowledge of the lives of the Desert Fathers, she strove to imitate their penances with her little group of friends and was tempted to flee into the desert. Later, in a dream, St. Dominic invited her to join his Order.

A very brief period of lukewarmness, instigated by the mother and to satisfy her older sister Bonaventura, was terminated by the sudden death of the latter and Catherine's "conversion." For the rest of her life she shed tears of regret over this brief period of slight vanity. She then cut off her hair and thereby made a clean break with the world and consecrated herself to God. After a great struggle, often harsh and violent, against the opposition of her mothers and brothers, she was admitted at the age of sixteen to the Dominican *Mantellate*, or tertiaries, who live in their own homes but wear the habit of the Dominican Sisters.[2] There followed three years of seclusion dedicated to recollection, domestic chores and works of penance done either at church or at home.

The devil unleashed tremendous forces against Catherine similar to the "temptations" of St. Anthony, Abbot; they never ceased tormenting her, and at times even striking her. However, praying confidently and humbly, and with works of penance, she always defeated him. Then there began, so as to conquer the desires of the flesh, a gradual reduction of nourishment and rest, to the point of a very singular type of life that was almost without food or sleep, that was, in the words of Blessed Raymond, "completely miraculous."[3] This period came to an end at the age of twenty, on Shrove Tuesday, with the mystical espousals with Jesus' gift to her of an invisible ring so that she was espoused to him in faith.

Her spiritual life, besides consisting of long vigils and extended fasts, is characterized by frequent reception of Communion and, in increasing measure, ecstasies and visions in which Jesus himself instructed and guided her.

Active Life. Spiritual Summits.

After the years of seclusion, the duty of charity drove Catherine out of the cell; her heavenly Spouse wanted it this way. First of all, she engaged in caring for the poor and nursing the sick, including those who posed more of a risk for her and those whose illnesses were repugnant. Then she engaged in spiritual assistance to prisoners, to those condemned to death, to sinners. Instrumental in some notable conversions that attracted the public's attention, she was regarded and sought out as a wonderworker.

Her sphere of influence grows larger as she reconciles various rival families in and around Siena. Solely out of respect for her religious habit, she is able to save the lives of her brothers during an insurrection. By now every kind of person has recourse to her for prayer and counsel, attracted by her miraculous powers, the charm of her virtues, but also by her wisdom and teaching. For someone without learning, she demonstrates a rare intuition of all that pertains to the spiritual life.

Among the more faithful of her followers, who call her Mamma, there are scholarly religious, Mantellate, young people drawn from the nobility and those who were cultured, who formed a particular family called by outsiders, with a degree of derision, the caterinati (the "catherinized" ones). They entrusted themselves to her, accompanying her on her missions of peace, serving as secretaries or scribes for her letter-writing. She guided them, prayed for them, followed them with her vigilant thoughts, and protected them from afar, offering to suffer for them for the expiation of their sins.

This spiritual maternity (that expanded beyond the confines of the city and state of Siena) resulted in the letters that she dictated, not knowing how to write, sometimes to several scribes at the same time and often while in ecstasy, in reply to those who had written her from faraway as well as to the disciples belonging to her "family," counseling, correcting, consoling, and spurring on every type of person.

In the midst of all this activity, ever multiplying and extending, there were also heavenly gifts (other than daily ecstasies and miraculous Communions) which were becoming more frequent and unusual. Among these we can enumerate some permanent gifts such as the ability to read hearts, the knowledge of things happening to her disciples when they were faraway, and similar things. There were other gifts which were occasional and connected to particular circumstances or events or to the progressive states of her spiritual life (such as the mystical espousals, mentioned above). Between 1370 and 1375 many mystical phenomena signaled her increasing spiritual maturity or called attention to the future tasks for which she was being prepared under the impulse of grace. As the reward for an heroic act, having drunk the bath water of someone with a festering sore, she drank at the wounded side of the Savior, which was repeated at other times, giving her a sense of intoxication from the divine blood, references to which fill her writings.[4] Likewise connected to particular circumstances (the patience to bear the slander of wagging tongues) was the choice of the crown of thorns that Catherine preferred to the crown of gold, wearing it, invisible yet painful, for her entire life.

The following events are connected to her spiritual growth: the exchange of hearts between the Savior and herself; the mystical death, which was a kind of foretaste of heaven, from which she would not have returned had it not been for a divine order and the fact that she was motivated by a sense of duty towards her disciples whom God had entrusted to her; the stigmata, received in Pisa on April 1, 1375, and that remained, at her request, interiorly painful but exteriorly only as luminous signs invisible to others.[5]

For Church and Country

Her constant flood of activity for peace and faith from individuals to families, from families to the city of Siena, from Siena to its environs, and from there to all of Italy and then to the entire Christian world, brought her ever further towards borders that were constantly expanding and to undertakings that she would never have dreamed of given her humble origins. Her activity is mingled with the politics of her time, not that she practiced politics but that every interest of hers in this regard was for the sake of peace, seeking "the honor of God and the salvation of souls" (letter 121).[6] "The entire war which is here will one day be extended over the infidels, raising the standard of the most holy cross," she writes to the *Signori* of Florence (letter 207). Her interventions in Church politics and the general problems of the Church were neither a presumptuous intrusion on her part nor a mania for action and moving about, but was always done because of obedience to the direct commands of God (see letter 219 *re* the cross and the olive branch) or to orders given by her by confessors, superiors, or the Pope himself.

The closer one is to God, the more one comprehends the need to return the gifts of God by being "useful to one's neighbor" for God. For Catherine, higher sanctity must always flow into the apostolate, according to the Dominican ideal.[7] The mystical life is intertwined with the active life. Her active life, in fact, began after the mystical espousals because the Lord wanted that she now cease her seclusion and would reach out to her neighbor. The summer of 1370 was, as Jorgensen says, "the summer of great visions" because of the importance of numerous divine communications culminating with the mystical death.[8] The visions become continuous, without suspending her usual penances; her fasting in Lent 1371, which lasted 55 days without any food whatsoever except for the Eucharist, attracted great attention. Her first letters regarding the public life of the Church and society were written in 1372

3

when Catherine was only 25 years old. Her activity for the Church and the world, now much vaster, developed as her mystical life became fuller.

The great religious problems that Catherine found before her were (see letter 206): the promotion of a crusade for the liberation of the Holy Land, the moral reform of the Church, and the return of the papacy from Avignon to Rome.

The *santo passagio* or crusade for the liberation of the Holy Sepulcher was the first great task that engaged her strengths along with those of her "family." This can be seen already in the first letters of 1372 that were certainly written after Gregory XI's bull on the crusade issued in the first year of his papacy. Her idea was that, besides liberating the holy places, the crusade would indirectly result in peace among Christians because it would either have distracted the forces of fratricidal war among the Christian powers, liberating them also from the affliction of mercenary companies (see letter 207), or because such a collaborative undertaking would be capable of cementing fraternal union among the Christian people.

In 1374 Catherine's promotion of the crusade was already so well-known that the master general of the Dominicans, perhaps during the Order's general chapter taking place in Florence, put at her side as a guide and director of her activities "for the salvation of souls, the crusade and other things regarding the Church" the learned friar Raymond of Capua; the choice was then confirmed by papal bull on August 17, 1376. For some years, until the Church was no longer convulsed by other more dramatic events, Catherine did not cease to exhort and goad all the powers-that-be to support this holy undertaking: kings and heads of state, ecclesiastics and noblemen, captains of mercenary companies, politicians and men of arms. Only the calamitous times in which she lived impeded the actualization of her plans.

The reform of the Church will always be uppermost in her thoughts and will inspire her eloquent and incessant appeals to anyone, from the Pope on down, who had responsibility or could contribute in anyway. The concept of her reform was to "clean the face of the Church,"[9] removing scandals and those who caused them, and "renovation," that is to say a moral reform, a return to the primitive spirit of the Gospels and to the initial purity of every religious institution. Reform is a matter that pertains exclusively to the hierarchical Church ("the mystic Body", as Catherine calls it) and cannot be entrusted to the laity or a secular arm because no one can touch the "anointed of Christ." The holy Church is the spouse of Christ. The principal instruments of reform in which the laity can participate are prayers, vigils, and the tears of God's true servants.

Such reform, starting from the interior to the exterior, must consist principally in the removal of bad pastors and putting in place good men at the head of dioceses and in ecclesiastical positions of dignity and in the return to the primitive discipline and simplicity in religious orders, which were in decline following the Black Death of 1348. Her spirit of reform, without any mitigation of morals or change in the Church's doctrine, would live on by means of her disciples, both immediate and indirect (Blessed Raymond of Cappua, Caffarini, Blessed Giovanni Dominici, Saint Antoninus Pierozzi, and Blesseds Chiara Gambacorti, Colomba da Rieti, and Osana Andreasi) and would bear fruit especially among the Dominicans.[10]

The return of the Pope to Rome and the Florentine struggle was the third great struggle she faced. From the time Pope Clement V moved to Avignon in 1305, the Holy See remained in France for over 70 years, with 1367-1370 being the only interruption when Urban V returned to Rome. The period was called the new "Babylonian Captivity." Great souls, such as St. Bridget of Sweden and Petrarch, and countless others, had implored the Pope in vain to return. The effects of the Avignon exile included the material and moral decadence of the Church and people of Rome and in the papal territories. The reaction of Cola di Rienzo, who set himself up as tribune of Rome from1347-1354 was a needed sign for the Pope to return. Other effects were bad governance by foreign legates, pastors and administrators and rebellions of the Romans, which were often bloody.

Inserted into this scene is the Florentine "War of the Eight Saints" (1375-1378) against the Pope. Moved by ambitions and egotism in Tuscany and by the fear of interference by the papal legates and the mercenary forces of John Hawkwood that were licensed by them, irritated by a refusal of a supply of grain during the famine of 1375, the Florentines entered into war against the Pope who, having offered a settlement, put the city under interdict and excommunicated its leaders. The magistrate of the "Eight of War" (called by the Florentines, ironically, the "Eight Saints") taxed the Florentine clergy for the costs of war and reconstruction. The republic drew in other rebellious Tuscan cities.

Catherine at first tried to limit the rebellion, holding back Pisa and Lucca for a while.[11] She then urged the Florentines to repent and make peace; finally, she was disposed to intercede with the Pope for their pardon. The collapse of trade and of their "banks," resulting from the excommunication, convinced the Florentines to negotiate with the Pope. Catherine, at the request of some of the governing authority, accepts to act as their ambassador of peace with the pontiff who knows and admires her.

She arrives in Avignon on June 18, 1376 and was quartered, with all of her "family," at the expense of the Pope. Her purposes, besides peace with Florence, are the return of the papacy to Rome and the crusade. She does not succeed in her peace plan because of the obstinacy and duplicity of the Florentines. She discusses the crusade with the Duke of Anjou. She insists on and argues for the departure to Rome, and reveals to the Pope a certain sign that it is the will of God and finally convinces him to do what he had promised and was prepared to do, having made a secret vow.

On September 13, 1376, the Pope leaves by ship with his fleet and court. Catherine goes by land with her twenty-two companions. They stop in Genoa where Catherine encourages the uncertain Pope to continue. While the "bella brigata" arrives in Tuscany, where they pause with their leader and "Mamma," Gregory XI enters Rome triumphantly on January 17, 1377.

The Last Years. Death and Glorification.

Two problems dominate the last three years of her life: peace with Florence and the great Western Schism. In the midst of these are inserted other minor initiatives, such as the renovation of the castle at Belcaro, given to her by the converted Nanni di ser Vanni, into the monastery of St. Mary of the Angels, and the apostolic mission in Val d'Orcia, with so many conversions that the three confessors authorized by the Pope to follow her everywhere are not enough.

In early March 1378, Gregory XI sends Catherine again to Florence to negotiate peace but he dies on March 27. After a tumultuous conclave comes the election and coronation of Urban VI, who confirms his trust in Catherine to negotiate peace. In June Catherine is almost killed in a riot in Florence (see letter 295). The riots stop and she writes to the new Pope imploring him for pardon and peace. In reply, on July 18 a messenger with the olive branch of peace sent by Urban enters Florence to the joy of everyone. It is peace. Catherine returns to Siena in August where she finishes dictating the Dialogue.

Schism bursts forth on September 20, 1378, with the election at Fondi of the anti-pope Clement VII. Catherine immediately takes the side of the true Pope and, on his orders, goes to Rome in November to fight alongside him. Received by him, she speaks before the cardinals in consistory. Her actions regarding the schism can be summarized as: (i) to support and encourage the true Pope by word, prayer and penance; (ii) to gather around him a good number of true servants of God; (iii) to send messengers and messages to every part to maintain or restore Italian and foreign powers in their obedience to the Pope; (iv) to fight the devil, who exacts revenge by striking and afflicting her in a thousand ways.

In her many labors she is literally consumed; she offers herself as a victim for the Church: "O God eternal, receive the sacrifice of my life in this mystical body of the holy Church" (letter 371). In her last days she will advise, "Keep firmly in mind, my sweetest and dearest children, that as I leave this body, I am aware of having truly worn-out and given up my life for the holy Church."[12] She went her to heavenly spouse, at the age of thirty-three, on April 29, 1380, after having exclaimed many times, "Blood! Blood!" She was buried in the basilica of Santa Maria sopra Minerva, where she now lies under the high altar; her head, however, was taken to Siena by Blessed Raymond in 1383.

The first sign of celestial triumph, which was spontaneous, were her funeral rites which attracted huge crowds. She was canonized, after long expectation owing to the problems of the time, by Pius II on June 29, 1461. Pius IX named her co-patron of Rome. She was also named a patron of Catholic women and of nurses in Italy. In 1939, Pius XII made her, together with St. Francis of Assisi, a primary patron of Italy. Finally, Paul VI, on October 15, 1967, announced his intention to give her, with St. Teresa of Avila, the title Doctor of the Church, which took place in St. Peter's on October 4, 1970.[13]

Inspired Teaching

St. Catherine, celestially inspired teacher, has left us her teaching in the writings and account of her life which have exercised, and are still exercising, considerable influence in Catholic spirituality.

The Works and the Life

The authentic Catherinian writings are the letters, the *Dialogue*, and the prayers. The inauthentic writing is the *Brief Dialogue,* otherwise known as the treatise *On Consummated Perfection* or *Devout Revelation.*[14]

The *epistolario* consists of 382 letters of various lengths written to every type of person, from popes to the most humble Christian, from kings and heads of state to simple manual laborers, and to ordinary women. All of the writings, or almost all of them, were dictated and only seven exist in their original form (in the hand of the copyist); the others are found in manuscript collections which date back to the time of her scribes, often without closing lines and greetings but essentially identical in text. Because of the editing and absence of the original texts (given the large number and quality of the correspondents, how was it possible to find them?), R. Fawtier introduced the first doubts regarding their authenticity but later recognized them in block.[15] They were defended by I. Taurisano and, above all, E. Duprè-Theseider who showed that, "The letters are, as a whole, authentic; considered individually, they do not seem to have been deformed or mutilated for ulterior purposes."[16] In fact, the mutilations, as we see from some rediscovered closing lines, were not made to falsify the letters nor to hide rough points or doctrinal errors but only out of concern for the persons mentioned who were still alive and only to conserve intact the text or body of the letter for edification and teaching.

Besides speaking of the great problems of her time, the letters illuminate all of Christian life and every grade and category of persons from which can be extracted a complete treatise on the spiritual life.[17] The letters are cited according to the numeration found in the edition of Gigli (Siena, 1713) and, better, in that of Tommaseo (Firenze, 1860), re-edited by Misciatelli (Siena, 1912 and 1921; Florence, 1939), and of Ferretti (Siena, 1918 and 1930) and recently of U. Meattini (3 vols, Edizioni Paolone, 1966). And in due course the critical edition edited by Professor E. Duprè-Theseider (first volume of 88 letters; Rome, 1940).

The major work, almost the longest "letter," which was dictated by Catherine, comes to us under various names: *Book of Divine Doctrine, Dialogue of Providence, Revelations* or *Book of Divine Revelation.* Catherine called it simply "the book" (see letter 373; other possible references can be found in letters 179 and 365). The time of composition is said by some to be longer and by others shorter; it is certain that it was finished before her departure for Rome, perhaps before the outbreak of the schism. It was dictated in Siena, in different sessions in 1378 in ecstasy, and dictated to three secretaries: Stefano Maconi, Neri di Landoccio dei Pagliarsi, and Barduccio Canigiani.[18]

There is no doubt that the work is substantially Catherine's even though there is no original codex (if there ever was one). There is some question as to whether her confessors may have made some interpolations or alterations, perhaps with Catherine's own authorization. To this we respond that the oldest codices go back to the same secretaries who originally transcribed them and are close in time to the original, before any type of rearrangement might have been made.[19] In fact, the division into chapters is not in the text but in the margins, and as such is different from other codices. Some disciples and translators were still alive at this time. The oldest codices are also independent one from the other, allowing for the possibility of resolving certain textual questions. The Latin translations, made early on by Maconi and Cristofano di Gano Guidini (another one of Catherine's secretaries) are most faithful to the text and do not contain any discrepancies of note. Such was the respect for the text, which was considered a revelation of God almost like Scripture, that the disciples would not have dared to alter it, especially if they had personally witnessed the actual dictation: "And I know one of those [times]," writes Cristofano, adding that he faithfully translated it: "I did it literally [in Latin], purely according to the text, without adding anything to it."[20]

There are diverse criteria for the division of the text of the *Dialogue.* First, it has been divided into treatises and chapters, which has the sole advantage of making it easier to make citations but, on the whole, results in much material that is not always logically placed or homogenous and which is not in the text nor from the one who dictated it. Another division of the text has been done according to Catherine's four petitions, but this is also insufficient because there are different parts of the work that do not fit into this schema. As a matter of fact, the book cannot be submitted or reduced to a single schema, rigid and pre-arranged, but rather to the free flow of question and answer. It develops around some central principles that, to a large extent, govern the entire canvass (the four petitions: for herself, for the Church, for the world, for a particular case; the tree of virtues; the allegory of the bridge; the work of providence and divine mercy); and around some themes dear to Catherine the spiritual teacher: divine mercy, the struggle of vices and virtues, the perfection of the human person according to the teaching of Christ, the dignity of priests and their reform, continuous prayer, obedience in general and obedience for religious.

Then, there is the collection of twenty-six prayers spoken while in ecstasy during the last months of her life and collected by her disciples. Not being a part of the preceding works, they are published separately as an *operetta* or little work of Catherine. They are ardent soliloquies, bursts of the soul, enflamed soliloquies with God, impassioned supplication, all full of both teaching and fire.

Finally, the *Life of St. Catherine of Siena* written by Blessed Raymond of Capua, her principal confessor from 1385 to 1395, is mentioned here because it presents us with the most authoritative testimony on Catherine's life and on the divine graces that produced this "miracle" of sanctity. Raymond recounts her most important practical teachings and their consistency with her personal way of living and sanctification. For a long time most of her teachings have been penetrated and understood in every field of Catholic spirituality through the vehicle of this biography. It is called the *Legenda major* to distinguish it from the "Legenda minor," an abridgement of it by Caffarini.[21]

Soul and Style

Many have written on this subject from the perspective of various aspects: literary, hagiographical, and mystical. As a classic of the Italian language and of mystical literature of the 14th century, Catherine is a teacher who continues to instruct, to be appreciated for her merits and loftiness, and to be increasingly known.

On Catherine as a spiritual writer, we note that she is not the author of dogmatic treatises nor does she discuss scholastic and speculative theses. She is not even an ascetical essayist, cold and detached, who expounds and schematizes theories. As A. Morta says in the introduction to his Spanish translation of the *Dialogue*: "Catherine does not write about what she knows. She writes about what she experiences. Better yet: she writes *what she lives*."[22]

Her asceticism, however, is always nurtured by doctrinal truth (the Trinity, the blood, the image of God in us) and by moral concepts based on the theological virtue of charity and connected to the other virtues. It trembles with passion but is not sentimental and it is directed to good actions without being moralistic. Her vision of things is on the mystical plane but is realistic, that is to say it is illuminated by He who has created and redeemed us, and projects us toward the full possession of him in eternal life. Her language, therefore, is extreme, without attenuation, as if from a divine source and with a direct thrust to the highest reality. The richness of allegories and metaphors is born from a need for concreteness and warms and colors a particular speculation or expression of the faith. The abundance of images may appear artificial and the absolutism of expression as a posture; rather, they are always a testimony of faith, of conviction and of lived experience, revealing her soul.

Influence and Judgment

As an important person in history, as a saint and teacher, Catherine has received praise and admiration in every field. Above all it is her biography which has become a classic in hagiography (despite certain weaknesses of its time) that has gained so much praise. Last of all, her writings and teaching, so widely diffused, merit the greatest fame of all.

Testimonies of her renown continue to increase. Among them we note the words of Pius II in the bull of canonization (1461): "No one approached her who did not go away better and more enlightened. Her teaching was infused, not acquired." The Dominican ascetical writer and preacher Louis of Granada (†1588) declares, in five discourses dedicated to St. Catherine: "I affirm that, after the ineffable mystery of the incarnation, I have read nothing that has offered me better proof of divine charity and goodness as the deeds of this virgin and the singular privileges God granted to her." The biblical exegete Cornelius a Lapide (Flemish Jesuit; †1637) described her with a well-crafted phrase: *"portentum omnium saeculorum"* ["a sign for all ages"].[23] Cardinal Sforza Pallavicini (Jesuit historian; †1667) concluded an octave in honor of Catherine preached in Venice in 1686 with these words: "After the Mother of God, I do not know of anyone who loved the King of Paradise as much as this virgin." Niccolò Tommaseo closes his long introduction to his reprinted edition of the letters with these words: "Great citizen, great soul, great writer."[24] Pius XII crowns these words of praise in the papal brief (1939) nominating Catherine, with St. Francis of Assisi, patron of Italy, referring to her as "an esteemed bulwark of Italy and religion."

In the last century commendations from the point of view of Italian literature have multiplied by historians and critics from every corner: Gaetano DeSanctis and Luigi Settembrini, Giosuè Carducci and Ruggero Bonghi, Giovanni Papini and Natalino Sapegno, Francesco Flora and Giorgio Petrocchi. We mention only a few among the more expressive: Gino Capponi, in his history of the Florentine republic, says: "It was a grave injustice not to have counted among the greats of the language of that age…Saint Catherine…who is a greater writer, and more truly noble and natural than Boccaccio."[25] Giovanni Papini, in his modern history of Italian literature, puts her among the leading writers of the 14th century, stating that "Catherine can indeed inspire, without seeking to do so, and is equal to the greatest."[26] Lastly, Jolanda DeBlasi is not afraid to assert that "next to the three greatest [of the 14th century: Dante, Petrarch, and Boccaccio] is, without hesitation,...Catherine Benincasa...." And later: "this illiterate ordinary woman...is the greatest of the Italian women writers and can be compared with the greatest writers."[27]

The spiritual influence of Catherine is seen in the history of spirituality in the centuries following her death where her deeds and words are diffused and arouse passion. We need only consider a few examples. Such was the influence in Italy on all religious that Pierre Pourrat could observe: "The Italian women mystics appear to be of much the same type as that of St. Catherine of Siena, whose biography was everywhere read with eagerness."[28] St. Teresa of Avila, who kept a list of saints to whom she was particularly devoted, recommended Catherine's example to her sisters. At her canonization process many witnesses declared that they had heard her say many times that, after God, she entrusted the direction of her soul on its way to heaven especially to Catherine.[29] A similar case, and also more accentuated, is that of St. Anthony Mary Claret who for his entire life was a faithful admirer and imitator of Catherine, often quoting her, recommending her to his religious, placing her from the beginning among the patron saints of the Claretians and always considered her as a teacher and director.

Not to be ignored is the vast influence of Catherine's influence among Protestants. Some of these, Lutherans (such as Gregorovius or Hase) or Anglicans (such as E. Gardner) or the Episcopalian Vida Scudder, are meritorious in their Catherinian studies. Others cite her frequently with respect in their works, such as Evelyn Underhill in her famous *Mysticism*, a classic on the nature and development of the spiritual consciousness of the human person, where, among other things, she says that Catherine "composed, in her *Divine Dialogue*, one of the jewels of Italian religious literature."[30]

By this time we can hear Catherine say to all her disciples near and far: "If you are what you should be, you will set all of Italy on fire" (letter 368). Indeed, the whole world.

CHAPTER TWO

KNOWLEDGE OF SELF

Although it goes back to the old *Know thyself* of the wise Greeks, the Catherinian theme of knowledge has a Christian character being as it is derived from St. Augustine ("Noverim te, noverim me")[31] and from traditional asceticism. It is not a fruit of introspection or pure psychology but rather it means entering into the human person as he or she is described by faith (created by God, fallen because of one's own fault and redeemed by the Son of God), considering the person from the perspective of the interior life of the soul more than in his or her outward history. According to Lemonnyer it is "a gift of grace, born from the consideration of our intelligence enlightened by faith"[32] and it has as its object both our misery and our natural-supernatural dignity. It is the fruit of faith that moves the intelligence to examine and humble itself, especially at times temptation. In the expressions of Catherine, knowledge at times is an interior grace, a light, a realistic consideration of one's own nothingness as creature and sinner in general; at other times, it is an examination and judgment of one's own faults for the purpose of humiliating, condemning, and correcting one's self; sometimes, it is the very act of self-humiliation, i.e., to recognize and to confess one's own misery.

How necessary the practice of self-knowledge is can be seen from the words of the Eternal Truth in the *Dialogue*: "One cannot attain virtue without knowledge of self and knowledge of me" (c. 43).[33] It is a fundamental necessity, not because of just some importance, but literally as the foundation of the spiritual life, that is say as a basic starting point of every virtue. "We must make a beginning based on knowledge of self and the knowledge of God in us" (letter 340). Because the soul cannot have two foundations (see letter 213), all other foundations are excluded and must be considered as false. Some false foundations are seeking one's own consolations in virtue; seeking visions and revelations;[34] corporal penances when considered as essential practices[35] and when they are instruments of the virtues—but not the virtues in themselves.

A true foundation of the spiritual life must be secure so as not to be subjected to diabolic illusions. It must be stable so as to last in time and in any state of health. It must depend on our will otherwise it is not meritorious and does not constitute a virtue, such as in the case of visions. It must not cause a person to become proud, as sometimes happens with fanatics and their exterior penances, but instead produce interior blessings. In fact, the true foundation is that which upholds the whole edifice of intrinsic or interior virtues at any time or in any place. Only the double knowledge of self and God in self can do this. The reason is that all the intrinsic virtues of the soul, namely humility and charity (from which all other virtues derive), depend on it. Because the whole edifice is founded on it, from the uppermost part to its depth, this foundation is active at all levels of the spiritual life, "this is the foundation, principle, means and aim of the commandments" (c. 54).

You are She Who is Not

"Do you know, daughter, who you are and who I am?," Jesus Christ once asked Catherine. "If you know these two things you have beatitude within your grasp." Here is how He himself answered this question: "You are she who is not, and I AM HE WHO IS."[36] Our definition as creatures is the opposite to God's definition of himself to Moses in Exodus 3:14.[37] Therefore, our fundamental discovery which must never leave our minds is this: at the root of our being, there is nothing of ours but only a gift of God who created us because of his goodness and redeemed us on the cross for the sake of love (see c. 4).

Radical Nothingness of the Creature

The creature is a contingent being before the All that is God, the absolute and unique being. This is true both in the natural and the supernatural order. In the natural order, because we are nothing by ourselves, having received everything, both our existence and nature: "I Am Who Am, and you yourselves are not; rather, you have been made by me who, the creator of all things that participate in being" (c. 18).

In the supernatural order, there is no gift that comes from us: "I Am He Who I Am, and they are those who are not; they have received being from my goodness and every grace that is placed over being" (c. 119). We can do nothing by ourselves if God does not give us the strength. We are unable to free ourselves from the least discomfort or from a disturbing thought: "by ourselves we cannot do any virtuous act, or be free from any battle or suffering; therefore, if we have any bodily infirmity or suffering or mental battle, we cannot take them away from ourselves [even for a moment]; in fact, if we could, we would take it away" (letter 23; see letter 335).

This consideration, which is neither pure philosophy nor a philosophical theory, which comes from Catherine's knowledge of Him who touched the naked depths of her own being, is the best answer to deceptive presumption and pride.

There is yet another reason in the moral order that aggravates our misery: sin. Sin is to oppose God because it consists in "loving what God hates, and hating what God loves" (c. 98), and so it deprives us of the right *to be*, of which God alone is the giver and Lord. "Being deprived of me because of his own fault—the Lord says—he [man] returns to nothing; I alone am He Who I Am" (c. 54).

Sin pushes the human person back to his or her radical nothingness, introducing a negative value, something like a right to non-being. In fact, Catherine defines it synthetically like this: "Sin is *non cavelle*," a Tuscan expression meaning "nothing," which is to say that it is the denial of good (as St. Augustine and St. Thomas Aquinas say) and the deprivation of grace, almost an annihilation of every right in the order of the natural being and of every power in the order of grace (see c. 94).

Indeed, sin reduces us to being "less than nothing" because it puts sinners at the level of beasts, having acted just as if they had no reason, i.e., depriving themselves of it. In this sense, Catherine says that the sinner "has lost the light of reason" (see letters 24, 149, 256, 362, etc.). Sin also takes away from us the right to life in every sense, giving to us the right to death and of eternal punishment: this seems worse than having in oneself "the condition of the animal" (letter 256).

It is worth remembering the devastation that sin provokes in the soul, being "the thing that is not" (c. 31):

> Alas, how dangerous sin is in the soul! It deprives man of good and makes him worthy of evil! It makes him worthy of death, taking the life of grace away from him; it takes away from him the light and gives him darkness; it takes away the lordship [=ownership of self], and gives him servitude. Thus, he who abounds in sin is servant and slave of sin;[38] he has lost his self-ownership allowing himself to be possessed by anger and other defects. (letter 149)

The mystery of sin is not yet wholly present. Catherine describes in strong terms the journey of the wicked toward damnation: they become unbearable to themselves (see letter 38; c. 96); in this they are given a foretaste of hell (ibid.); and, in spite of knowing it and tasting it, they do not want to turn back and thus one could call them "martyrs of the devil" (cc. 48, 51). This is a paradoxical expression which depicts effectively a foolish position.

In conclusion, to understand the scope of this monstrous situation one must only return to "self-knowledge with a holy consideration; that is, thinking of who the person who offends God is, and who God, the one offended, is" (letter 362).

Temptation, too, is useful in knowing ourselves; in this, the devil himself becomes a useful minister of God's mercy. God has two main purposes for allowing temptation (see c. 43; letter 335): to test and exercise virtue (this reason relates, above all, to self-knowledge), and to provide an occasion for growth in grace and merit (see letter 335).

As far as the first reason is concerned, it is not God who needs this but ourselves. In fact, to prove that a given virtue is or is not present and efficient in the soul, it is absolutely necessary that the conscience be awakened and stimulated because it can so easily deceive itself and fall asleep owing to the way things appear to it. Testing and exercising the virtues also serves to consolidate oneself in doing good because every virtue is proven and fortified by its contrary (see c. 43), that is, by temptation of the opposite vice.

The testing and exercising of virtue results, above all, in an interior light of knowledge. One's possession of this light, in fact, is in exact proportion to the possession of virtue or lack of it. One comes to know better his own weaknesses and, therefore, sees the necessity of humbling oneself by turning to God for help so as to avoid a fall. It is good here to note that the perfect are also tested so that they may be given opportunities for merit, as well as "to keep them in knowledge of themselves, from which they draw true humility. This makes them compassionate and not cruel toward their neighbor.... But those who have more compassion have more feeling for those who suffer, than if they had not suffered" (c. 145). This interior light of knowledge, the result of the testing and exercising of virtue, is so clearly shown as a specific grace coming from one's being tested that we can now also see the goodness of God in allowing it:

> One cannot attain to virtue if not through knowledge of oneself and me; this knowledge is acquired more perfectly at the time of temptation, because it is then that [man] knows that he is not, being unable to be freed from the pain and disturbance from which he would like to flee, and he knows me with his will [which is fortified through my goodness in such a way] that he does not consent to those thoughts. (c. 43)[39]

Concerning the second reason for temptation, i.e., growth in faith and merit (see letter 335), we must know that the soul obtains the best "gains in times of battle" (letter 62). We must not flee the battlefield because, "He who does not fight does not have victory" (letter 169). We must not forget the doctrine of the inviolability of the will, which St. Catherine takes from St. Thomas and St. Antony the Abbot.[40] This truth is a source of consolation and stability for the one who is tempted. In fact, there is nothing to be afraid of because evil and good require the consent of the will which is such a well-built "fortress" that neither the devil nor any other creature can enter it and compel it to consent unless the will wants it. It is up to us not to place the will by the "hand of free will" into the hands of the devil but to keep it united to the will of God (cc. 43, 144; letters 28, 335, etc.).

We acquire a defense against temptations after making an act of humility and confidence in God, with the weapon of prayer which must never be set aside. When the trial is stronger and lasts longer, then some acts of mortification are also necessary. Another defense is good thoughts so as to occupy the mind, not giving room to thoughts of the devil, and not setting ourselves in direct opposition to him.[41]

In all of these ways, the nuisance of temptation obtains for us again "the little virtue of humility through knowledge of self and the virtue of charity through knowledge of God, which are the two wings that make the soul fly to eternal life" (letter 335).

Fruits of Self-Knowledge

The most important fruits of self-knowledge are: *humility*, self-knowledge being essentially the recognition of our nothingness and worthlessness: *self-hatred*,[42] so as to fight the enemy of self-love, which is more tenacious than humility and self-knowledge; *penance*, so as to rise up from the misery of sin.[43]

Humility

We will say more about this virtue in Chapter Four when we treat of the tree of charity, because St. Catherine assigns to humility two contemporaneous tasks: to precede every other virtue after the birth of self-knowledge and to nourish charity, like soil in which the tree of charity and every other virtue take root. Here let us look at it particularly in relation to knowledge of self.

Humility is the first fruit of self-knowledge because it comes forth from the same motive of knowledge, that is the awareness of one's nothingness in the order of nature and grace. This means that humility is truth because it comes immediately from knowledge, i.e., from a real vision of oneself: "we shall never reach the virtue of humility if not through a real knowledge of ourselves" (letter 23), and from a sincere recognition of our own misery and littleness to the extent that humility is as wide as the circle of true self-knowledge (see c. 63), no more or less. It also means that, compared to the other virtues, humility has an absolute precedence and a fundamental indispensability: "Every perfection and every virtue proceed from charity, and charity is nurtured by humility, and humility flows out of the knowledge and holy hated of oneself" (c. 63).

Humility consists in the abasement of one's self-esteem. Catherine imaginatively describes it (see c. 10; letter 363, etc.) as ground or soil, circumscribed by self-knowledge, at a lower level so as to form a depression, the "valley of humility," protected "between two strong mountains, that is between the virtues of fortitude and true patience" (letter 363). It is called "the little virtue" (letter 23; c. 159) because it consists in making ourselves little according to the Gospel dictate,[44] bringing down pride and presumption; but actually it is a very great virtue because it animates the entire spiritual combat against the soul's enemies and sustains the entire edifice of the virtues.

Humility has positive and negative aspects. The negative aspects pertain to the elimination of all that opposes the sense of my nothingness.[45] Humility nurtures self-hatred, above all the hatred of our own sensuality tending to the only thing that is ours, the nothingness of sin. Humility, coming from self-knowledge, destroys the roots ("the beards") of pride, "seeing that we have nothing to be puffed up about" (letter 185; see letter 366). It combats the presumption of the one who "wanted to climb before descending," presuming to know and judge the mysteries of God without first knowing oneself: "If we want to see the stars of his mysteries, let us enter the deep well of true humility" (letter 343). Humility runs away from vain-glory and supports us when we are despised: "The vein of humility comes forth from this knowledge; it is never concerned about its reputation, and is not scandalized by anything but suffers every injury with patience and joy" (letter 49). Finally, it lowers and submits us before every creature for the love of God (letter 61), reducing us in our relation with our neighbor before God.

Humility in its positive aspects nurtures and supports the other virtues. It is the "soil" in which the tree of charity and every virtue sink its roots; this is possible after the "beards" (roots), i.e., the subterranean motives of pride, are destroyed by sincere self-knowledge. Humility is also the "wet nurse of charity" (letter 366), rendering nourishment to the tree of charity (see c. 10), like soil with the tree's roots in it, and by this means it nurtures and moderates the other virtues such as patience and obedience. Patience is "the marrow of the tree" (c. 10) of charity (see letter 355) that grows inasmuch as humility grows: "as much as one is humble he will be patient, and as much as he is patient he will be humble" (letter 23). Obedience, which is not possible without the submission produced by humility, is similar: "One is obedient as much as he is humble, and is humble as much as he is obedient" (c. 154) to the point that "in the soul which does not have this little virtue of humility, obedience immediately dies" (c. 159).

Humility is acquired, first of all, "with a true knowledge of ourselves, with hatred and sorrow for our own sensuality" (letter 365). Then, by considering models of this virtue; above all, the humility of the spotless Lamb which not only inspires but gives the value of life-giving energy, like sap, to all our virtues.

Since God humbled himself before man by giving us this sweet and loving Word, and, since the Word of the Son of God, with true patience, humbled himself in obedience unto death, death on the cross, our justice and every virtue have value[46] through his humility... (letter 363)

Is there anything more striking than to see God humble himself before man? To see the supreme loftiness descend to such lowliness?[47] (letter 345; see letter 79)

Immediately following the example of the Son is the humility of the Virgin Mary: "The virtue of Mary's humility pleased God so much that, through his goodness, he was compelled to offer to her the Word of his only begotten Son; and she was such a sweet mother as to offer him to us" (letter 38).[48] Finally, there is the example of the saints who "wanting to make an exchange [to the Son of God who humbled himself before man], were constantly humbling themselves, giving all praise and glory to God" (letter 177).

Self-Love and Holy Self-Hatred

The greatest enemy of knowledge and humility, in the line of the visible and cognitive, is self-love or self-will which consists in keeping our eyes turned too much to ourselves; in the line of the affective, it is an excessive attachment to our own views, desires, passions and satisfactions. Self-love can take two forms:
First, there is *sensitive self-love* (or sensuality) which is the egoism of the senses, the search for all that concerns material or physical life (earnings, pleasures, affections):

If sensitive affection wants to love things that can be grasped by the senses, the eye of the intellect focuses on them and thus takes transitory things as its sole object, with self-love, disgust of the virtues and love of vice from which [the soul] draws forth pride and impatience. (c. 51)

Sensitive self-love "proceeds from pride and, therefore, it contains every evil in itself" (c. 17). It is the trunk of the deadly tree of sin, rooted in pride and with the marrow of impatience (see c. 31).[49] It makes us fearful and afflicted solely because of our material losses.
Second, there is *spiritual self-love* which is a form of egotism that sees and performs virtuous acts inasmuch as they are useful "for our own personal utility or delight or pleasure." It causes us to suffer and go away from all that is good when there is no more satisfaction or advantage for ourselves.[50] Some signs of the presence of spiritual self-love are given in letter 263:

- Preferring one's own consolation and quiet rather than helping one's neighbor;

- Preferring an act of personal devotion to an urgent but less pleasant work of mercy;
- Having a spiritual friendship which results in suffering because of jealousy or because our love is not reciprocated;
- No longer praying when we are busy with many other things or when we do not get what we wanted after praying for it.

The evils that the soul derives from sensitive self-love are basically two. First, the damage caused by self-love will be seen in the arresting of our journey towards perfection.[51]   Second, self-love in general, and above all sensitive self-love, is at the origin of all disorders and sins. "You know," the Lord said to Catherine, "that every evil is founded on self-love, and this love is a cloud that takes away the light of reason" (i.e., the good use of reason; c. 51). In particular, self-love, in working like a cloud that covers the eye of reason and the pupil of faith, does not allow the soul to look at itself in self-knowledge; it hinders our judgment and the right evaluation of things "so that bitter things taste sweet, and sweet things taste bitter; it blinds the soul and does not allow it to know and to discern the truth" (letter 315); it causes the soul to neglect spiritual exercises at the time of temptation (ibid.) and doing good for our neighbor; it spurs the soul to exempt itself from obedience through a false judgment (ibid.).   In summary, it exposes the soul to many deceits and illusions

Self-hated is the logical solution to the continuous assaults of self-love, and it comes from true knowledge: "This knowledge generates sorrow and hatred of sin, as well as for one's selfish sensuality" (c.4). The evangelical foundation of hating one's own sensuality is found in the words, ""Whoever comes to me and does not hate father and mother, wife and children, brothers and sisters, yes, and even life itself, cannot be my disciple" (Lk 14:26); and Jn 12:25: "Those who love their life lose it, and those who hate their life in this world will keep it for eternal life."

In the notion of self-hatred there is a contradictory opposition, made to balance evil with good, opposing holy self-hatred to perverse self-love: "Two contrary ways of love cannot stay together; we need to be stripped of perverse love and clothed with the love of God" (letter 287).   How does this come to be? "With the holy hatred of ourselves as we know our own faults" (letter 173).

There is yet an absolute extremism expressed already in the word *hatred*: it i a matter of mortal hatred against all that causes us mortal harm.

I want each of you to make two parts within yourself, that is sensuality and reason, and that they be mortal enemies. Reason must be armed, taking the knife of hatred and love. This war is not meant to be fought slowly but with effectiveness, managing to kill it [sensuality] at any cost because whatever takes away from us the life of grace must be killed. (letter 332)

Resolute and decisive ways are needed for a struggle so extreme: "You need to cut it off and not just untie it. Because whatever is not cut off remains connected" (letter 205). Knowledge, therefore, must be both judge and executer of justice so as to kill this perverse will, "and the way of killing it is this: to mount the chair[52] of our conscience, and to keep reason in it [=in delivering the sentence]." "And never let the least thought outside of God pass without correcting it with great reproach" (letter 265).

Here is the needed weapon: "the knife of hatred and of love. "Let man make two parts of himself, that is sensuality and reason, and let reason take out the doubled-edged knife, namely of hatred of vice and love of virtue, using it to keep sensuality as a servant, uprooting every vice and movement of vice in the soul" (letter 265). Hatred and love unite, or better still are allied, so that we may not think that the Catherinian ascetical norms are solely negative and therefore inhuman but rather to show that the two-edged knife is not there so much to destroy as to build up the edifice of virtues which, through knowledge, must rise up from the valley of humility. Let us understand that Catherinian asceticism, in this heroic war against self-love, consists of fortitude and virility. This killing of self-love, "cut off with the knife of hatred and love, that is with hatred of sin and love of virtue" (letter 314; see letters 62, 159, etc.), will have a repercussion throughout the progress of our spiritual lives.

Penance

We have mentioned how the awareness of sin can result in humble knowledge of our human misery and spiritual combat against our sensuality. Sin and interior struggle are two real elements of life. They recall a third, one that we have already mentioned but intentionally left out in our consideration of the foundation but which must have its place here after self-hatred as a means of struggle and liberation: penance.

We need to distinguish the interior virtue of penance and the exterior practices of penance, also known as mortifications or corporal penances. The first thing we must notice with our teacher Catherine is that interior penance is a true virtue, whereas corporal or exterior penances are means or instruments of the virtues, meant to exercise and increase them (see cc. 9, 11); letters 210, 340). Those who care only for corporal or exterior penances would not be virtuous and tending to perfection. Those who put their confidence, therefore, in exterior penances deceive themselves, acting as if these were the essence of the spiritual life. These penances kill the body, but not the will if they are not accompanied by interior virtues: Catherine says that "they cut the weeds, but do not uproot them" (letter 213). They sometimes weaken the body and may also lead to discouragement if they have to be interrupted or are not practiced with discretion. Exterior penances can generate the presumption of virtue in those who have the physical capacity to make the effort, and can lead to murmuring and judging those who are unable to do them as if they were outside the way of perfection. Lastly, due to an excessive attachment to them, those practicing them become disobedient toward their confessors or superiors.[53]

The virtue of penance, on the other hand, must be born from self-knowledge, namely from the vision of one's own misery and the discovery of our worst enemy, self-love. It must be inspired by self-hatred and hatred of sin: "with very much hatred for offending God and love of virtues" (letter 276). It must be aimed "at killing one's will and mortifying the body" (letter 340), because "perfection does not consist just in lacerating and killing the body, but in killing one's own perverse will" (c. 104). It must try to destroy in both soul and body every trace of sin, "uprooting every vice" (letter 265) and without neglecting any immediate correction, any movement contrary to the virtues (ibid; letters 21, 315, 321, 361, etc.; cc. 60, 73). Finally, the virtue of penance includes offering reparation to Christ crucified for one's own faults, almost blood for blood, vengeance and satisfaction (letter 4).

It remains to be said that we have no need to despise or abandon corporal penances that repair in the flesh the sins of the flesh: "so that, because of the perverse law of the flesh that fights against the spirit" the bodily members may not be dragged to moral disorder of the senses, they are mortified in various ways provided the exterior penance serves as an instrument to exercise and develop the interior virtues and that, regarding time and manner, every practice of bodily mortification must be ruled by discretion (see letter 213).

In conclusion, penance and self-hatred, nothingness and humility, sound like negative concepts and proposals made to deny or destroy the positive truth of our being. However, if this were true we would only be looking at things super-ficially. Knowledge is not fake knowledge: it is the recognition of a correct appraisal of what we are, i.e., that we are nothing by ourselves, so that we might not build our life on a false presupposition. Penance is not suicide but a means that prevents us from trying to be what we must not be. To found our life on truth is the purpose of both knowledge and penance, as we have already seen. On the other hand, to have a complete concept of the human person, in his or her dignity and social and ecclesial dimensions, the other knowledge which we will speak about in the next chapter is necessary. "We could not see our dignity and our defects in any other way except by way of going to look at ourselves in the mirror of the peaceful sea of the divine Essence" (letter 226).

CHAPTER THREE

KNOWLEDGE OF GOD IN SELF

Knowledge of self and of God is as one, like the negative and positive aspects of our reality which cannot be separated or put together in wrong order. In fact, the spiritual principle of knowledge is only one: "We must make one principle of knowledge of ourselves and of God in us" (letter 340). It would be disastrous if the first were without the second, because the soul would remain dejected, depressed and desperate (see letter 23); and would fall into pride and presumption if it remained only in knowing God's goodness in us (ibid.; see c. 73; letters 51, 73, etc). I do not know whether Pascal knew this Catherinian theory when he wrote the following thought:

> The knowledge of God without that of man's misery causes pride. The knowledge of man's misery without that of God causes despair. The knowledge of Jesus Christ constitutes the middle course, because in Him we find both God and our misery.[54]

There is, moreover, an order between the two that cannot be changed: the knowledge of oneself must always precede the other, just as the night (that is, the knowledge of oneself) must precede the day (the knowledge of God) and not vice-versa. That is to say, we who are born into nothingness must first acknowledge our poverty and then we must pass on to understand God's goodness in us. Humility, which is born from knowledge of self, is the "wet-nurse" of charity, which in turn is born from the knowledge of God, as the former predisposes one for the latter (see letter 365). "He who does not know oneself cannot know me" (letter 272).

Once we understand what knowledge of self is, it is time to make "a cell not built by hands,"[55] as Catherine admonishes us: "Make for yourself a cell in your mind from which you can never leave" (ibid). What is this cell, which is one of her most characteristic images? This is how she describes it to Alessa Saracini:

> Make, my daughter, two dwelling places: one actual dwelling place of the cell so that you may not go about talking in different places except if it is necessary or because of obedience to the prioress or because of charity. And another dwelling place that is spiritual, which you carry with you constantly: and this is the cell of knowledge of yourself where you will find the knowledge of God's goodness in you. They are two cells in one [=two types of knowledge united] and, by being in one you will want to stay in the other, otherwise the soul would be led to confusion and pre-

sumption. (letter 49; see letters 94, 104, etc.)

Distinct from an actual monastic cell, the cell of knowledge is a mental cell, as it is expressly called in another place: "because before you leave behind your material cell, you have already left behind your mental cell" (letter 37). This is not a mental fiction but a habitual attitude of the mind. In this sense it is also called "the cell of the heart" (letters 215, 373), a place of interior recollection.

The activity that takes place in the cell is entirely spiritual; e.g., "the intellectual vigil" of the eye of the mind that scrutinizes "the deep thoughts of the heart" (c. 63); the watch dog of conscience which protects the entry way into the city of the soul and barks at all intruders (see c. 129); "the judge who sits on the seat of conscience and who judges," rules and moderates (letter 358); continuous and holy prayer, perseverance in which attains to the perfection of charity (see cc. 63-66). In summary, the cell is a habitual capacity of entering into oneself, discovering oneself in one's own interior reality. It verifies the conviction of one's own humility. It assures us that our own journey unfolds in the light of faith. It is to converse with God, enjoying his intimate presence.

The strict connection between faith and knowledge helps us to understand the preeminence of faith in the Catherinian spiritual conception, which is dominated by the visible element resulting from both. She speaks of knowledge as a phenomenon of interior light, an intellectual fact but not purely rational since it involves both reason and faith (see letter 301). It is a seeing of the intellect illuminated by faith (see c. 45). Existentially speaking, reason and faith are like the eye and its pupil, for the sake of knowing: "The true eye of our soul is the intellect which has the light of most holy faith" (letter 151), and "the light is the pupil of the eye of the intellect" (letter 284; see c. 45).

Faith and knowledge have the same object, God, who is always defined according to revelation: "I am He Who I am"; "I am God, Love" (letter 146). The importance and necessity of both, always united, results from the necessity of "having the light" so that one does not "go into darkness" (letters 64, 318). It is also from the fact that, just as the cognitive act is not verified in the human person if the eye of the intellect does not see, so the intellect does not understand divine truth if it is not illuminated by the light of faith (see letters 87, 301, 199). Furthermore, it also results from the necessity of growing concurrently in knowledge and faith so that baptismal grace, which "would not be enough if we do not exercise the light of faith with love" (letter 122), matures in us. Thus, baptismal grace seeks, through the exercise of knowledge that leads to the development of faith, such spiritual maturity that reaches in this life to an anticipation of the beatific vision and "the pledge of eternal life" (cc. 45, 85).

Faith and knowledge have joint functions. Together they are a single point of departure for going along the way of virtue and a single foundation which was excavated and built on the site of knowledge and in the light of faith (see letters 199, 340, 345, 366, etc.). Faith and holy knowledge also keep us constantly on the "way of truth," which is the way that truly leads to salvation: "without the light we cannot go along the way of truth, but we will go in darkness" (letter 64; see letter 284). Lastly, they allow us to find ourselves in God and God in us, even in this life:

> That is to say, you found yourselves in him, having created you in his image and likeness, not out of any debt but by grace; and in ourselves is found God's immeasurable goodness, having taken our likeness through the union that he made of divine nature with human nature. (letter 226)

Let us conclude by showing here how Catherine animates all the mysteries of the faith:

> We must therefore have the light, as I have said, and keep to the way of knowledge of ourselves and of knowledge of the goodness of God in us, with hatred of vice and love of virtue. This is a road and a house [=cell] where the soul knows and learns the doctrine of Christ crucified. In this house of knowledge of ourselves and of God we will find the face of our soul washed clean. (letter 87)

I Am He Who I Am

God Is All

The purpose of the affirmation of the radical nothingness of the creature is to highlight the absolute transcendence of God in being and power and in his goodness and providential action in us. Let us consider some general affirmations concerning this point. First, God is all and there is nothing that does not come from him: "We must believe, and not so much believe but be certain, that he is, and that everything that in itself has being comes from God, except sin which is nothing" (letter 13). Second, in the line of being and acting, nothing natural or supernatural can take away from his creative power and justice (see c. 18): "they have received their being from my goodness and every grace beyond being" (c. 119). Even now nothing escapes his influence: "I am He that I am, and nothing is done without me, expect sin which is nothing" (c. 46). Third, He "has no need of our good" (letter 199) and nothing can be added to him: "He is our God who has no need of us, but we have need of him because without him we can have nothing" (letter 362). We, therefore, cannot be of any direct use to him but we can and we must be of use to our neighbor for love of him (see cc. 7, 46; letter 226, etc.). Fourth, he is like a "peaceful sea" that cannot be contained by any vessel (c. 165), "from which comes everything that has being" (letter 30) and in which is immersed every existing thing, particularly the soul in grace, penetrated as it is by his divine action: "As the fish is in the sea and the sea in the fish, so I am in the soul and the soul in me, the peaceful sea" (c. 112).

The Goodness of God in Us

We must, above all, know the Creator in his relations with us "because in the knowledge that the soul has of itself it knows God better, knowing the goodness of God in it; and in the gentle mirror of God, [the soul] knows its dignity and its own indignity" (c. 13).[56] In this mirror we see the reflex of what happens in God himself, when seeing oneself and the reflex of love join hands: "When I looked inside myself, I was enamored by my creature and was pleased to create it" (c. 135). We note in particular:

God created us out of love, and therefore, his love always precedes us. God loved us gratuitously before we existed (see c. 143; letter 28), love alone "constrained him to create us" (prayer 17/X).[57] We love when we are loved, but, as Catherine says: "You loved me without first being loved by me" (c. 108). As he has created us, so he also conserves us through love: "my love created you and my love conserves you" (c. 82).[58] Before we were his friends he atoned for our sins: "Your love for us is worthy of commendation; that being your enemies, you have given us life and paid the price of your blood for us" (letter 184). God is "He who loves without being loved" (letter 77). His grace precedes and produces every meritorious action: "Of every favor done for you, you are the operator and donor.... This is what your boundless love does: you want to reward us with your love" (letter 66).

His love for us is universal and differentiated, in other words it is offered to all men and women without any distinction ("God extends his charity to the just and sinners," letter 94), but then it seems to adapt itself to return the measure of our love: "With that love with which I am loved, with that love I respond" (c. 60), and so it appears to us "some he loves as a son, some as a friend, some as a servant, and some as one who has left him and whose return he desires" (letter 94).

God loves us with a merciful love as vast as he is, infinite, insuperable: "Is he not quicker to pardon than we are to sin?" (letter 178). The same love with which he created us now constrains him to have pity on sinners (see c. 143), a pity without boundaries: "My mercy, which you received in the blood, is incomparably greater than all the sins committed in the world" (c. 129).

To sum up, the reason and motive of every gift that God gives us is his love: the whole history of the mysteries of the faith, from creation up to the present, attest to it and from which it follows that "love has made all things" (letter 47) and that "everything that God has made and makes for us is made because of love" (letter 184).

Providence

God wants nothing other than our good (see letters 77, 97; c. 140). The love that prompted him to create us also moved him to destine us for eternal happiness; and he pursues this purpose in his governing the world in all its aspects and in his actions toward us, in particular in granting us the gifts of nature and grace, the virtues and the gifts of the Spirit (see c. 140) and the remedies necessary for our infirmities (see letter 48). His love is manifested in permitting the tribulations and ills of life, the persecutions, the temptations, and the trials of every kind, "granting to us the fire of love" (letter 25) so as to purify us and lead us back to the way that leads to eternal life (see c. 141, etc.).[59] He also does this by taking care of each of us, according to circumstances; in fact "the goodness of God continually works in us" (letter 23). He takes care of every person: sinners (see c. 143), to whom he gives the stimulus of their conscience in order that they will implore his mercy; imperfect souls, to whom he gives the trial of aridity in order that they will improve (see c. 144); perfect souls, cultivating their souls with different tribulations in order to grow in perfection (see c. 145).

The Trinity Itself and in Us

St. Catherine, so as to help us increase in knowledge of self and of God, puts in relief the two principal mysteries of our faith from which come a better and more truly Christian knowledge of God and ourselves: the holy Trinity and the redemption. Like every other truth, Catherine does not expound the whole of Catholic doctrine concerning these mysteries, presuming its integrity, but she insistently calls attention to those aspects that lead her nearer to the mystery, as seen in the mirror of her own soul and in the illuminating light of her knowledge.

The Eternal Trinity

The eternal Trinity in itself is the divinity in concrete, with a well defined face which emerges from revelation; above all, it is the deity, as seen by faith, at work in creation and in ourselves. It is the definitive divine reality present or reflected in us, or mirrored in the soul. The unity of divine nature ("one and the same sun", c. 110), the distinctions of the Persons and the order in which they subsist, are truths which Catherine affirms in line with perfect Catholic faith and the most genuine theology.

At the origin of all things, the Trinity, moved solely by "uncreated charity," creates the world and the human person (see c. 13). Particularly in the creation of man and woman it seems that "the whole Trinity consented" (prayer 1/I), as if a specific communication of itself to us (ibid.; c. 13). The same can be said of the general working out of providence, particularly in the history of the fall and restoration of the human race (see c. 135). Providence is an attribute of the whole Trinity in the guiding of humanity and all of creation to its proper end: "Everything was made by my providence, and so, I tell you, it will continue to provide up to the very end (c. 137).

Above all, Catherine considers the three divine Persons in the line of mediating functions through which the divine action reaches us. Indeed it seems that the Persons operate in us by mediating the qualities common to the Trinity (power, wisdom, and clemency or love), attributing or appropriating them to a single Person (see cc. 13, 110; prayers 3/III, 13/IV) so as to give us a formal participation in them (see prayer 1/I). Also, the divine missions of the three Persons to believers come in the same order and with the same qualities: "So he came…with the power that is appropriated to the Father, and with the wisdom that is appropriated to the Son, and with the benevolence and love that is appropriated to the Holy Spirit" (letter 94; see cc. 63, 135).

The Trinity is sought by the soul that is sincerely oriented in its affections toward God, and the soul gives itself to the Trinity as the terminus of love in this life in response to the hidden interior visitations effected by the three appropriations mentioned above (see c. 61; see c. 29). These visitations are a preparation and an anticipation of beatitude, i.e., the vision of God in heaven. Perfect souls somehow have a foretaste of it in this world (see c. 78), but only the blessed in heaven actually reach "the height of the Trinity" (c. 83).[60] God gave to the human soul the participation of the three Persons, as he says, "solely for the reason that it would be able to understand and taste me and enjoy my goodness in the eternal vision of myself" (c. 135). Catherine says that we could not comprehend our dignity "if we did not go and see ourselves mirrored in the peaceful sea of the divine Essence" by means of the way of knowledge (letter 226), and so that she sees the Trinity as a very high road which has no end: "so it seemed it was a road of the greatest height, the eternal Trinity, where we receive so much light and knowledge of the goodness of God that we cannot express it" (letter 226).

The Created Trinity

The image of God in us is like a created trinity that leads us to know, by an instinctive reflex in us, the uncreated Trinity. The Lord created us not only in the *image* of the divine unity but also in the *likeness* of the Trinity of three

27

Persons (see cc. 13, 51, etc.). This likeness is in the human soul, which is one in the essence and trinity of the soul's powers of memory, intellect and will and therefore has "the form of the Trinity" (prayer 1/I), resembling the unity and Trinity of God (see prayer 3/III). These three powers, being a participation in the three divine Persons in the sense of appropriation, make us similar to them and unite us to them according to these attributions (see prayer 3/III; cc. 4, 13).

This created trinity (but Catherine does not use this expression) is a living reproduction of the uncreated Trinity since it is made in the likeness of the soul's powers,[61] not in some static sense that would be only an imitation, diagrammatic and skeletal, but in a dynamic and purposeful sense in as much as the three faculties are oriented towards God:

> Thanks be to you…for having shown us so much love, giving us the sweet form and powers of our souls: namely, the intellect to know you; the memory to remember you and to preserve you in us; the will and love to love you above every other thing. (prayer 1/I; see c. 135)

Here Catherine, having followed St. Augustine in enumerating the soul's powers, intuits and welcomes the Thomistic clarification that better responds to her realistic and concrete mysticism.[62] Having seen the correspondence between the soul's three powers and the three divine Persons it is easy to pass to the three theological virtues and to see the correspondence of the trinitarian image in the moral and supernatural order of grace. But the argument is barely touched on by Catherine (see c. 131), while, as we have seen, the three appropriations recur often: power to the Father, wisdom to the Word, and clemency or love to the Holy Spirit, which are also ways in which the Trinity communicates itself to us (see prayer 3/III).

The perfection of this created trinity will consist in the perfect imitation and complete union with the eternal Trinity. In the formal sense, this perfection consists in the union of the three powers, firmly gathered together in the name of God and full of the benefits received from him (see cc. 54-55). In the objective sense, it consists in seeking the Trinity with a desire to *see* the three Persons in their light, seeing ourselves mirrored in them; to definitively *confirm* the soul, immersing it in the peaceful sea of the Deity and unceasingly penetrating further and further into his "abyss of charity"; to *taste* eternal life in the sweetness of being an image of the Trinity, fully responding to it and being clothed in it (see c. 167).

The Blood of Christ in Us

So that we might arrive at "perfect knowledge" of the goodness of God in us, faith tells us that the Deity has come down among us thus realizing the mysteries of the incarnation and bloody redemption:

> For that sweet will, with which he created us to give us eternal life, was not fulfilled because of our sin; for this reason he sent his son to make it clear and evident, giving him over to the disgraceful death of the cross. (letter 122)

It is obvious that, for Catherine, Christ, the Word incarnate, is the manifestation of the Father's love, above all by the blood shed on the cross which becomes a source of life for all men and women. Let us now examine this theme of the blood.

The Incarnation

The incarnation, however, is not simply a point of passage to the bloody redemption, even though Catherine constantly says that the reason for the descent of the Son of God to earth was to remedy sin. But we cannot deny that the incarnation is the necessary complement of the redemption. In fact, the Word became flesh by the force of love and as a proof of love:

> God the Father, constrained by the fire of his charity, sent us the Word of his only Son, who came like a chariot of fire, manifesting to us the fire of ineffable love and the mercy of the eternal Father, teaching us the doctrine of the truth, and showing us the way of love, which we must hold to. (letter 35)[63]

Such proof of love was required by the condition of sinful humanity which, owing to original sin (see cc. 14, 21), rebelled against God through disobedience which resulted from pride (see c. 154), was blind and deprived of knowledge of self and of God's goodness in oneself (see c. 46), and who was incapable of reaching eternal life through its own good works. The incarnation, therefore, was an act of merciful love and a revelation of divine goodness: "because of the mercy and inestimable love I have for man, I sent the Word of my only-begotten Son" (c. 166). Thus the goodness of God is found in us to such an extent that "man is made God, and God is made man" (cc. 15, 110). Catherine can say to the Lord that, through this union "we are your image, and you are our image" (c. 13).

Catherine insists on the reality of the two natures in Christ who is "all God and all man" (c. 110), because only the union with divinity gave infinite value to the actions and sufferings of Christ for us (see c. 14). "You must

29

know that if he had been pure man without being God, the blood would have no value" (letter 73). This is a fundamental truth on which all the subsequent notions concerning redemption, salvation, and our life of grace are founded.

The incarnation has put the incarnate Word as our *head* under which all people are gathered together, because as our knight (see letter 256) and captain he fights for us and wins (see letters 64, 71, 97, etc.; c. 100) and therefore all of us must follow him. He is our head because he is the fount of every grace from which all must draw. He is also our only *mediator* (see letter 71; c. 13) and only bridge (see letter 272; *Dialogue*) able to unite earth and heaven (see c. 22). He is the *stone* on which all the true virtues, like living stones, are built, i.e., all the virtues are founded and sustained by the grace and charity of Christ so much so that "there is no virtue that is not tested in him, and all the virtues have life from him. Therefore, no one can have any virtue that gives the life of grace but from him" (c. 27).

From the viewpoint of example and moral teaching, in Christ are found written all the virtues (see c. 154) as if written in a book, among which Catherine underscores especially the miraculous example he left us of abasement and humility (see letter 79), as well as the example of obedience illuminated by love and filled with it (see c. 154; letter 84) and, last of all, the example of patience (see letters 101, 151, 226, etc.; c. 154)

All of this comes to the fore above all in the consideration of the blood poured out for us on the cross.

The Blood of Christ

St. Catherine drank repeatedly at the side of the Savior and was soaked by a shower of blood and fire.[64] Her communions left in her mouth the taste of blood. By virtue of these mystical experiences, all her writings were colored with blood. Every letter begins with this salutation, "I write to you in his precious blood." Given the vast extent of the usage she made of it, let us look at the different senses this word has in her language. However, so that this analysis will not be taken in a purely superficial or literary sense, we warn that one reaches the blood, in all its fullness of meaning and value, through the charismatic way of knowledge of the faith: "In this house of knowledge of self and of God we find the blood" (letter 87).[65] The blood is the point of convergence of all the mysteries; from the creative Trinity to man's final end everything is seen from this point of view. The blood, therefore, is a complex reminder of all that faith and life in Christ means, as well as of the whole meaning of Christian asceticism and mysticism.

The blood manifests to us the most important truth, namely the love of God for us (see letter 9, c. 305, etc.). Catherine presumes the dogma of the redemption and so she does not expound it doctrinally but prefers to identify the principal argument more suited to prove this truth, namely that God loves us and wants us to be happy with him in eternity.

The truth that God loves us with an immense love, like an infinite abyss, is demonstrated by the blood "shed with so much fire of love" (letters 304,307) removes every doubt about the reality of this divine love (see c. 13), "the abyss of his inestimable charity" (letter 51) because "only through the fire of love" has he bought us back with the blood, not having any actual need of us (see prayer 17/X). Even when we became his enemies through sin, God loves us and wants us to be saved:

> What manifests to us this truth and this love? The blood of the humble and immaculate Lamb.... If God had not created us for the end that has been said, and did not love us inestimably, he would not have given us such a Redeemer. (letter 9; see letters 13, 78, 193, etc.)

God also loves us in our adversities, because he cannot allow tribulations out of a lack of love or so as to lose us, but to better save us: "What shows [God's love] to us? The blood. If God had wanted another thing for us, he would not have given us the Son, and the Son would not have given his life for us" (letter 25).

The truth that was most hidden to us regards God's real will to save us. It is now confirmed for us in the blood. There is "an eternal truth: that we were loved before we existed" and that God "created us so that we might participate in him, and enjoy his eternal and supreme good. Who has declared and manifested this truth to us? The blood of the humble and immaculate Lamb" (letter 305).[66] This is what Catherine calls "the truth of God the Father" (letters 102, 195, 227), i.e., the secret of the Father, and therefore only the Son, Word of the Father, could reveal it to us: the will to communicate to us "his eternal beauty" (letter 102), that is to give himself to us in eternal life. We must realize the fact of God's will as being true and that it constitutes a truth that can be believed. "But because of man's fault this truth is not being fulfilled in him; and so God gave us the Word of his Son" (letter 193). The incarnation is a great mystery, yet its truth seemingly was not adequate for the Father's charity and the manifestation of the truth. "Was this union [of the divine and human] enough for your charity towards [humanity]? No, it was not, therefore, you eternal Word, watered this tree with your blood" (prayer 21/XV). The definitive proof of the truth is the sacrifice of Calvary, the offering of blood that seals a solemn commitment of the divine will, incontestable confirmation that God wanted "to manifest his truth in his blood" (letter 93). Therefore, "this truth is not hidden from us; the blood manifests it" (letter 9) and has made it dramatically tangible: "O glorious life-giving blood that has made visible for us what is invisible, that has manifested to us the divine mercy, washing away the sin of disobedience with the obedience of the Word, from which the blood has come forth" (letter 55; see c. 66).

The obedience shown by the incarnate Son, up to the point of blood and death, also confirms the same truth which is both "ancient and new:" "the blood manifests this prompt obedience" (letter 315) accomplished by Jesus who was "drunk with love for the eternal Father and our salvation" (ibid.). The Father "commanded him through obedience that he put his blood in the midst of us, so that his will might be fulfilled in us and we might be sanctified in the blood" (letter 36).

The immense value of the price paid to redeem us and the abundance and warmth with which it was given testify to the mercy of the Father and the love of the Son who "like someone in love, ran to pay the price of his blood" (letter 81) "with such starving desire and inflamed love," and, Catherine says in another place, "the suffering of desire is greater than the suffering of the body" (letter 34) so that "from every part [of his body] poured out" blood out of which he makes a bath for us (c. 151).

And so we arrive and discover the "secret of the heart," a discovery of love of which we will speak later, and "in this knowledge of self [you] will know my mercy in the blood of my only-begotten Son" (c. 63). Every truth is illuminated by the blood, like a raging fire, in which blood and fire, redemption and love, become one and the same thing (see letter 102; see c. 127): "and this union was so perfect that we cannot have fire without blood, nor blood without fire" (letter 189). The most precious blood becomes a synthesis of knowledge or illumination, an angle from which to view the principle truths of faith: "Therefore," concludes Catherine, "look at yourselves in the mirror of the blood, that you may find in this vessel yourselves" (letter 153), where "to find" in the blood means to recognize in it a new instrument in which to know the truth.

The Blood Represents Grace

The blood opens to the eye of the soul the entire invisible world of grace in as much as everything depends on it and has its source and nourishment in it. In the word "blood" the world of grace has its embodiment and its most lively expression. "In the blood we have life" (letter 153). The frequent use of the words "in the blood" tend to include all that St. Paul intended when he said "in Christ," i.e., all the truths to be believed and the virtues to be practiced, all the promptings of the Spirit, all the sure ways of sanctification (see

32

letters 102, 124). In the blood we see the grace of the redemption in itself and in us.

Catherine expresses *the grace of the redemption* in its state as a well-spring which is a purifying and spiritually transforming fount. The entire value of the blood resides in the hypostatic union, which Catherine even calls "eternal blood," as well as in the infinite value of the price of our redemption "by virtue of the eternal Deity, the infinite divine nature" (c. 14), in addition to the sense that it was decreed from all eternity and leads to eternity, and hence it is never consumed: "O eternal blood, eternal I say because you are united with the divine nature" (prayer 20/XIII).

"In ourselves we find the blood that manifested the love that God has for us; in the blood we receive our redemption and are recreated in grace. We are that vessel that has received the blood...." (letter 304). The mystery of our redemption is seen constantly in its actualization through blood. First, the redemption is seen as a new creation in the blood: "in his blood we find that he has recreated us in grace" (letter 259); "through love we are recreated by grace in the blood of Christ crucified" (letter 263, etc.). Second, the redemption is seen as the grace of spiritual rebirth: "God wants the child of human generation to be reborn in the blood" (letter 259). Lastly, it is seen as here-and-now graces given to every generation that receives the fruits of the redemption so that Catherine often speaks of it either in the eternal present appropriate to the divinity or transfers herself and us to the past making us contemporaries with the mystery:

> We are that earth where the standard of the cross was fixed; we are like a vessel which receives the blood of the Lamb that ran down from the cross.... So then we are that earth that keeps the cross upright, and we are the vessel that receives the blood. (letter 102; see letter 223)

The multiple effects of grace are described with a great variety of words and images which are impossible to catalogue but can be grouped under three headings: the blood of Christ is *the purifying cleansing from every stain of sin* for which Catherine uses all the verbs that express the action of liquid: the blood washes, irrigates, floods, soaks into the mortar, stains, colors, pours, runs, bathes; above all, the invitation to bathe in it which Catherine considers an indispensable element for the cleansing of the entire person. The blood is a liquid that can be drunk because it gives life and quenches the thirst of pilgrim travelers on their way toward heaven (see cc. 27, 66). *The blood is the means of liberating us from the slavery of sin* whether as breaking the devil's chain ("With his blood he removes servitude to sin, and makes us free, drawing us away from the lordship of the devil" letter 112; see letter 189) or as medicine that heals us from our ills (see letter 168): "He has healed our wounds with his blood" (letter 126). Finally, *the blood is the key that has opened the gates of heaven for us* (see c. 27). The key of "obedience to the Father" was thrown into the mud by Adam and was useless and rusted, until the Son of God repaired it through his obedience, "washing it with his blood" (c. 155).

We cannot comprehend the Christian created in grace if we do not know the meaning of his or her life. This life, which is *the life of grace in us,* is characterized by the blood; in fact, "in the blood we have life" (letter 153), which echoes Jn 1:4, "In him was life." The definition of the Christian for Catherine could be: body, soul, and blood. In fact, in her perennial invitation to self-knowledge, she says: "In that knowledge you are found to be a vessel which receives this glorious and precious blood" (letter 153). Let us examine the various elements of Christian life so as to understand the life of grace contained in the blood.

Christian life has its source in these components. First, the divine Trinity which is found "in this blood through the union of divine nature and the human nature." Second, the physical humanity of Christ represented by the blood which flowed from it. Third, God's charity for us which "was the bond joining God with man and man with God; it kept this Word nailed and fastened to the wood of the most holy cross" (letter 153). Christ is the fount of living water because of the blood shed by his wounds, and from it "we draw the water of grace" (letter 318).

The formal element or *essence* of this life is the "light of grace," the seed of which we receive in baptism and which we must make to bear fruit in this life by remaining engrafted with the true vine that is Christ (see c. 24). "The light of grace" is a gift that comes to us from the Holy Spirit "in virtue of the blood" and, together with light, warmth, and color (which we experience in the sunlight) we have a participation in the Sun that is God the Trinity (see c. 119). The "light of grace" makes the soul a heaven (see c. 33) because God lives in it (see c. 51). It recreates us to the life of adopted sons and daughters of God (see c. 60), and makes it possible for us to reach, in as much as he dwells in us, eternal life (see letter 122).

The life of grace is manifested in the virtues; the blood *gives value to every virtue* (see letter 363). This affirmation, repeated often by Catherine, is not just a mystical theory but a true description of the Christian virtues: "because they are all ripened and watered in the blood" (letter 355). That is to say, the true and real virtues are those that not only correspond to the philosophical definition of virtue but also lead us "to the gate of eternal life, the gate that is unlocked by the blood of Christ" (letter 345). These virtues depend essentially on a vital bond of faith and grace with Christ without which they lose all value: "every virtue has value and gives life when it is founded on Christ and drenched in his blood" (letter 181). These virtues, which Catherine compares to stones made to construct the bridge between earth and heaven, were not embedded in this bridge before the passion of Christ and so no one "could reach his end [=heaven]," and because "heaven had not yet been unlocked with the key of the blood." However, once the passion was accomplished Christ "planted them like living stones, cementing them in with his blood, so that every faithful one may go speedily" to life (c. 27). The concept here is clear although it is veiled under an image. Another image used for the same purpose is the garden of the soul that has grown wild and uncultivated because of sin, but after the redemption is "a garden drenched by the blood of Christ crucified" which produces "fragrant flowers" of the virtues (c. 140).

The *sacraments* are life-giving conduits through which the life of grace comes to us (see letters 168, 171). Like every other supernatural gift, they "all have life and value for us in virtue of the blood, if we receive them with a true and holy disposition" (letter 339; see cc. 115, 119, etc.). Whenever priests administer the sacraments it is in fact the blood that they administer to the faithful (see c. 23), which we call prosaically sacramental grace. It is necessary to make this clearer so as to know how Catherine describes the extent of this life-giving fruitfulness.

We have already said that *baptism* gives us the first grace. It comes to us from the wounded side of Christ (see letter 189; see c. 75). Only in virtue of the blood does it take away the stain of original sin and give us the life of grace (see cc. 14, 75, 135). When it is a baptism of fire (that is, of desire), "it is not without blood, because the blood is drenched and kneaded with the fire of divine charity, having been shed out of love" (c. 75). We notice how, for Catherine, the blood is always presented in its essence whether she is speaking of the baptism of water, blood (as in the case of the martyrs), fire, or of blood and fire (see c. 75).

Penance is a "baptism of blood and fire" (letter 189) that can be used every day as medicine for our daily infirmities (see letters 28, 102). This magnificent expression means the descent of divine love and pardon as a gift of the most precious blood that produces effects similar to that of "re-baptism" as regards personal or actual sins (see letters 102, 358). Penance can also be called "a continuous baptism of blood which one receives with contrition of heart and with holy confession" made to the priest in which "blood is cast, in absolution, over the face of the soul" (c. 75) or "upon our head" (letter 155; see c.140). "Every time that man comes out of the guilt of mortal sin and receives the blood in holy confession, we can say that he is born anew every time" (letter 305). This is a continuous proof, under our very eyes, that the Lord wants us to participate in his supreme goodness (letter 305; see letter 189).

It should not have to be said that the *Eucharist* is the "sacrament of the body and blood of Jesus Christ," that the two things are inseparable (c. 110; letter 208), and that it contains both the soul and divinity of Christ, "all God and all man" (c. 110). Without wanting to call to mind all that Catherine says of this august sacrament (which is the Catholic doctrine on the subject), her eucharistic experiences and her advice and defense of frequent communions (see letter 266), we note that her attention is turned in a particular way to the blood in Holy Communion in which we receive "his body as food and his blood as drink" (c. 110) as nourishment and comfort for life's wayfarers (see c. 27).

"That thing which gives life, namely the precious blood of the only begotten Son" (c. 14) "endows the soul with every grace" according to the dispositions of the one who receive him but "does damage to the one who receives communion unworthily, not because of some defect in the blood or the minister, but because of one's evil disposition" (ibid.) The table of the Lamb appears to Catherine like "a table pierced with holes, full of veins that sprout blood" by means of a "channel [=the opened side of Christ] that gushes out blood and water mixed with fire," sign of an inexhaustible communication of grace and love in which "the secret of the heart" is discovered (letter 208).

Catherine affirms that the reality of the eucharistic presence is not nullified by the unworthiness of the recipient or of the minister, although the fruit of its grace is forfeited (see c. 110). Only the eye of faith can see in the Eucharist "God and man," "the abyss of the Trinity, all God and all man" (letter 266), and "the soul's feeling" perceives it and the "palate of the soul" savors it (c. 111).

Body and blood, soul and divinity are like a sun within the sacrament (see c. 110) that is never consumed when one receives it but once the species are consumed "the imprint of grace" remains in the soul like a seal that imprints on it the characters of the Trinity (c. 112).[67] Nevertheless, a stupendous communication has occurred because the soul, as the Lord says, in "receiving this sacrament is in me and I in her as the fish is in the sea and the sea in the fish, so I am in the soul and the soul in me, the peaceful sea" (c. 112).

It is here that the eucharistic blood becomes inebriating wine (see letter 208) for the ecstatic communicant, which Catherine often devotes some time to describe according to her experience, the "sobria ebrietas" (inebriated sobriety) of which the Church Fathers and the mystics speak. It is the phenomenon of ecstasy caused by communion or by intense meditation and is similar in some of its effects to the inebriation caused by too much wine: "and acts like someone who drinks too much, who is drunk and loses himself" (letter 208; see letters 25, 75, 124, 263).

Now we can better understand the often repeated Catherinian invitation: "Drown yourself therefore in the blood of Christ crucified, and bathe yourself in the blood, and inebriate yourself with the blood, satiate yourself in the blood, clothe yourself in the blood…" (letter 102).

Holy Orders confers to priests the highest power and dignity because they consecrate the blood and administer it in the sacraments. With the Eucharist and Orders we are at the heart of the economy of grace[68] which Catherine describes in reference to its source, i.e., the blood that invests the entire Church with sacramentality: the Church is "a wine cellar [*cellaio*] in which was found the blood of the only-begotten" (c. 115). Priests and Popes have the office of "administering the blood" (ibid.) and so they are called "ministers of the blood" (cc. 117, 127) and also "ministers of the sun" (c. 110) for the honor they have of administering the sun of the Trinity with "the light of learning [and] the warmth of charity," and above all because they consecrate the sacrament of the Lord who with "his sweetest blood is a sun, all God and all man" (ibid.). Priesthood and blood are so identified with each other that if the priest were to betray his ministry he likewise betrays the blood (see c.113); to revere the priest is to revere the blood (see c. 116); to persecute the blood is to persecute priests (see cc.116-117). The same is said of the Pope: "Anyone who despises this sweet Vicar despises the blood…because they are joined together" (letter 171).

Prayer is an essential coefficient cause of the necessary life-giving energy for the Christian and is also linked to the blood.[69] Grace, this vital energy, is given to us when we implore God to "weigh the price of the blood of his Son" (c. 134) and give us the fruit of his Son's blood. When we ask for things that conform to God's will, grace as well as all the fruits of the blood are granted to us. This is true especially if we ask for spiritual graces:

> This is the blood that your servants ask for, like hungry beggars at the door. They are asking you through that blood to show mercy to the world and make holy Church blossom with fragrant flowers of good and holy pastors and with this fragrance to drive away the stench of the evil and putrid flowers. (c. 134)

Thus Catherine comes out with this precise affirmation: "The blood is ours" (c. 134; see letter 193), which is to say that we have a right to ask and to obtain from the Father all the graces that this Son has merited and acquired for us with his blood.

The Blood Signifies the Doctrine of Life

Jesus Christ reveals to us the "way of truth," i.e., his "way of doctrine" (cc.29, 166), a way that was opened and marked out by the blood (see cc. 27, 100; letters 83, 173, 315): "the road is beaten down in the blood of my Truth" (c. 135; see letters 29, 271, etc). This statement must be underscored because of the dramatic way with which it is put forward and for the heroic soul of the "virile combatant" who requests to follow it, as seen here: "we are placed on this battlefield and we must always fight" (letter 114) and "he who does not fight does not have victory" (letter 169). A characteristic trace of a christological and soteriological mark which Catherine insists on many times is her statement that we must go to the Father by means of Christ crucified, i.e., through the way of suffering: "in me, [the eternal] Father, no pain can befall me; but pain can befall my Son. And you, while you are pilgrims and wayfarers in this mortal life, you could not travel without suffering because through sin the earth brought forth thorns" (c. 53; see letters 318, 272, etc.).

We find the doctrine of truth in Christ crucified. From the cross, like a *cattedra* [sic],[70] he has taught us "the doctrine of the truth and ...the way of love and the doctrine of the truth" (letter 35), intending that his bloody sacrifice is the true "way and our rule"[71] that he wants to give us from a high *cattedra* so that all might know it (see letters 101, 216, 316). Christ is the glorious book where are written all the virtues (see c. 154), a book written "not with ink but with blood" and also "with large letters so that no one, even if he has little understanding, can be excused" from not comprehending it (letter 316; see letter 309). Christ's wounds are the blood-red paragraphs of this book where he explains to us the progressive path that we traverse on the way of truth, rising from Christ's wounded feet (by crucifying our sensual affections) to his side where we "find the warm-hearted love of the true and real virtues in the open heart" and then to the head crowned with thorns, where the will (our head) is crucified and we taste peace. Last of all, there are the pierced hands of Christ where we learn to do every good work according to God's will and for the good of our neighbors (see letter 309).

The memory of the blood is the bath in which we can continuously immerse ourselves and obtain every kind of benefit, such as: the sweetening of bitter things and the lightening of burdens (see letter 260); animating us to "give blood for blood" (letter 143) and to fight and win against temptations with trust in the merits of the crucified Christ (see letter 261; c. 66); extinguishing in us the fire of the flesh's sensual passions (see letter 21); provoking in us hatred for the enemy who killed our Lord, i.e., sin. The memory of the blood is the motive that justifies and prompts in us every virtuous act: "The memory of the blood in us gives warmth and light to cold and darksome souls, giving such largesse and removing stinginess; removing pride and infusing humility; taking away hard-heartedness and giving piety" (letter 210; see letter 167).

Faith, hope and love are found in the blood of Christ (letter 56, etc.), but above all in the way of love that we find "in the blood of Christ crucified, who shed it out of love on the wood of the most holy cross" (letter 297). It is not a love of sweetness or feeling but a love of immense dimensions by which we must measure our loving response.

Catherine does not have words to qualify God's ineffable, inestimable, and boundless charity for us and so she refers to the Gospel: "greater love he could not show us (this is what he said) than to give one's life for his friend," indeed "he gave his life for his enemy" (letter 196).[72] Certainly we recognize the greatest expression of this in the shedding of the "blood of Christ crucified, in which more than anything else blood, the largesse of inestimable charity is shown to us" above all because it benefits us who were once his enemies through sin. "This exceeds every love" (letter 184).

As far as its intensity is concerned, divine charity seems to exceed every visible medium and fails to express itself completely even in the sufferings on the cross. The divine desire for our salvation is infinite and does not exhaust itself in any manner of corporal punishment, which in itself is finite (see letters 8, 11, 12, 34, 16, 185, etc.). This is why the blood and the fire are united, as we saw. Far greater than his physical pain was the pain of Jesus' desire, the expression of which is found in wanting the last thrust of the lance and the shedding of his last drop of blood, signifying that he loved more than he could give:[73] "through the opening of [Christ's] side I showed you the secret of the heart; for there was within [Christ] even more of my affection for man which was not shown by the external body and its actions" (letter 189).

Here is "the way and the doctrine and the rule" that Christ crucified gives to the perfect and imperfect souls, and seems to say to us: "Here I have made for you the way and opened the gate with my blood. Therefore do not neglect to follow it" (letter 64). This boundless example is our "rule of love" to which we must give our heart: "Therefore he has truly given you the rule of love, showing you greater love than you could show him, giving life to you who were enemies to him and to me, the supreme and eternal Father" (c. 151).

In conclusion, everything must be known, seen, and evaluated "in the blood" and then everything in this life must be sought and dared, completed and perfected "in the blood," that is, according to Jesus' teaching, example, style and measure, the highest demonstration always being found in the sacrifice of the Savior.

Between God and Ourselves:
The Church and the Blessed Virgin Mary

In this panorama of knowledge, i.e., the Christian vision of ourselves and of God's work in us, two realities are to be found: the Church and Mary, both of which are part of Christian life and of our relationship with God. Let us look more closely at this scene.

The Church

The mystery of the Church is the reality in which and by means of which we see God accomplish his desire to communicate to us his infinite joy and beauty; and we, children of the Church, know ourselves to be cooperators in God's designs in fulfilling the truth of the Father.

From the perspective of the desire of God—but the schema could equally be seen under the profile of providence or of divine mercy—the mystery of the Church, as seen by St. Catherine, is described in three lines of thought.

First, the holy desire of God is the "truth of the Father," that is to say his intention or will that we be made participants in his eternal joy (see cc. 13, 21, 140, etc.).[74] This desire is confirmed, after original sin, with the counsel of the Trinity to send the Son to incarnate and sacrifice himself for us (see prayer 21/XV). Second, the Son comes to earth to show us this truth and to fulfill it with his blood. The thirst of the Son's desire, of love of the Father and for our salvation, accompanies the Son throughout his life (see letters 11,16) like an interior cross more painful than any other. Above all, this truth was revealed and realized in his torment during the passion, as was demonstrated when he says, "I thirst" (see letters 8, 12). Third, this pain of the cross of desire in Christ comes to an end with his death, but the desire itself does not cease (see letter 11) because "holy desire never ends," otherwise everything would have ended for us (see letter 16). It lives again in souls such as Catherine's, "made anxious with the greatest desire for God's honor and the salvation of souls" (c. 1) and in the Church to which the appeal "I thirst" is addressed and to which Christ communicates the "strain of desire" (letter 11), this thirst for the honor of God and the salvation of souls (see letters 8, 12, 16, 36, etc.)

The Lord has assigned the task of prolonging his desire through the centuries to his servants, whom he calls his "Christs" (cc. 116, 133; prayer 23/XVI), who may or may not be his ministers. To the Church he has left his blood, the expression of his love and of his anxiety as Savior: "The treasure of the Church is the blood of Christ, given as the price for the soul" (letter 209). Cooperation in the apostolate, to which God calls everyone in the Church, binds together in one purpose the vine grower who is the Father, the vine that is the Son, and we, the branches engrafted onto him (see cc. 23-24), according to the well-known Gospel allegory (Jn 15:1-6).

In her teaching on the mystery of the Church—leaving aside definitions or ecclesiological treatises, which were never Catherine's intention—we must note *the Church's solidarity* with Christ and among the members of the Church. In regard to its solidarity with Christ, whatever is done to it is done to him (see letter 171). "The Church is nothing other than Christ" (ibid.) and he is its Head (see c. 89; letter 207). In regard to solidarity among Christians, who are members of his body the Church, God calls them, "my people" (c. 13). In the Church and from it, the members receive life as branches engrafted onto the true vine which, when detached from it because of sin, decay (see c. 24). This solidarity of the whole body is expressed in the allegory of the three vines, i.e., the soul, the neighbor and the Church (see letters 313, 321), from which it results that, in order to cultivate one's own vineyard, one must work also for the other two which are united to it by many common bonds: the fountain of grace, the blood that waters the vine, the tree of charity that extends its branches over the entire field, and the principal vine grower who is "Christ on earth"[75] to whom, in a particular way, "the bond of holy obedience joins us, without which our vine would be ruined" (letter 321).

Then there is *the Church's sacramentality*, being as it is an indispensable instrument for salvation, which has a twofold meaning. First, through its function as a mediator between Christ and ourselves: "we cannot have salvation if not in the mystical body of holy Church, whose head is Christ and we are the members" (letter 207); the Lord said, concerning the Church: "Know that you cannot have desire for the salvation of souls if you do not have it for holy Church because she is the universal body of all creatures who participate in the light of holy faith and cannot have life if they are not obedient to my spouse" (letter 282). Second, the Church is a living reality in exclusive relation to the blood, being "founded on the blood" (prayer 5/XXIV), as "the wine cellar where is found the blood of the immaculate Lamb" (letter 306; see c. 115) that "holds in itself the blood of Christ" (letter 171) which is its truest "treasure" (letter 209). Therefore, the Church is the dispenser of the sacraments and, for its members, the fruits of the blood (see letter 171; cc. 27, 66, etc.).

We note *the Church's institutional form* in which are distinguished, according to Catherine (see c. 23), the "mystical body" that in a restricted sense indicates the clergy, the ministers of Christ, placed by God to "pasture your souls, administering to you the blood in the sacraments" (c. 23; see c. 7, 12, 14, etc.) and to teach doctrine and by example (see letter 191). This is to be distinguished from the "universal body of the Christian religion," that is to say the faithful, who are called to work in the vineyard according to their state (ibid.) at the very least by their prayers and obedience. Lastly, between the "mystical body" and the "universal body" is found a third category which belongs above all to the charismatic character of the Church: states of life and "servants of God." The states of life, in particular the "holy religions" or religious orders, that are "made and founded by the Holy Spirit" (c. 125) and seek "the great perfection," the actual observance of the evangelical counsels and the commandments (c. 47).[76] The "servants of God" (also called "his Christs"),[77] raised up by the Lord among people of every state, with the task, above all, of offering prayers, hard work and tears to obtain mercy for the world and the reform of holy Church (see cc. 15, 86, 166, etc.).

Finally, we note the *Vicar of Christ*, the "sweet Christ on earth" (as Catherine often calls the Pope, associating him with Christ's passion for the Church), is unique in the persona and the powers that he has received from God alone. "He has the power and the authority and nobody can take them away from his hands because they are given to him by first sweet Truth" (letter 28). He has in his hand all the powers of the Church (see letter 218) so "that which he does is done; and that which he does not do is not done" (letter 171). In particular, he is the cellarer, the guardian who "keeps the keys of the blood" (letters 305, 309), i.e., not only the keys of heaven by which he opens and closes the gates of eternal life (see letter 171), but also because the sacraments (which have value in virtue of the blood) are, directly or indirectly, "all administered by him and without him no one can receive them because he keeps the keys of the blood of the humble Lamb" (letter 339; see letter 207). Therefore, more than temporal things or his ruling over cities, he must devote himself to pasturing and saving all the "many sheep that are the Church's treasure" because they were acquired with the blood of Christ (letter 209).

The lay faithful and the ministers are all "bound to the vineyard of holy Church" (c. 23) under its head worker, the Pope, bound with the bond of holy obedience (see letter 321). They "cannot have life if they are not obedient to the spouse" of Christ (letter 282) and to its head. To him, Christ on earth, the Lord gave the key of obedience so that we must all obey him "and he who is outside of his obedience is in the state of damnation" (c. 154).

The Blessed Virgin Mary

Writing at the beginning of all of her letters the words, "in the name of Jesus Christ crucified and of sweet Mary," Catherine shows that she always wanted to place Mary immediately after Jesus. Let us summarize in a few lines what Catherine has to say.

Mary is the meeting point between God and earth. In fact, she is the field in which the Word was sown and she who has "given the flower of sweet Jesus" (letter 144) to us. Taking flesh in her and from her, the Son of God was engrafted onto humanity or humanity was engrafted onto him (see letters 77, 138, 144, 183, 242). Having had God dwelling in her, she was made the "temple of the Trinity" and, having conceived the incarnate Word through the work of the Holy Spirit, Catherine calls Mary "the book in which our rule is written" by the "hand of the Holy Spirit" (prayer 21/XV).

Mary "buys back the human race" (ibid.) because the flesh of the Word, that was born of her and was somehow her flesh, bought back the world by suffering on the cross (ibid.). Moreover, in her soul Mary cooperated with the work of human redemption, standing at the foot of the cross with a perfect and heroic conformity of sentiments and intentions with her divine Son, moved by the sacrifice of the Father's love and by her desire for our salvation. In the Father and the Son "this boundless desire was so strong" (letters 144, 342) that the Son ran to his death out of the great love that he had so as to give us life; the hunger, the great desire of holy obedience to the Father was so much that he lost all love of himself and ran to the cross. This same thing is done by our sweetest and dearest Mother who voluntarily loses the Son's love. (letter 30)

That is, she puts aside her natural instinct of motherly love: "not only does she not behave as a mother, in that she does not deter him from death, but she wants to make of herself a ladder" (letter 30) so as to cooperate in the fulfillment of the Father's will, thus being able to "put her Son on the cross, if there had been no other way" (letters 144, 342). Catherine attributes this paradoxical expression to others: "so say the doctors" (ibid).[78]

Mary is the Mother of Grace and the "Bait" of our Salvation.

The reasons for devotion to Mary are based on the certainty of her maternal intercession for us, on its power and efficacy, and on the imitation of her virtues. Mary "is our advocate, mother of grace and of mercy" through whom the Son of God once came and comes forth from her forever like a "chariot of fire," the Son of God with his "fire of love" for us (letter 184).[79] This is more than sufficient reason to serve her with filial affection: "She is not ungrateful toward those who serve her; rather she is grateful and thankful" (ibid.).

"I know that nothing is denied you, Mary" (prayer 21/XV), Catherine confesses in perfect agreement with Catholic doctrine. The power of her intercession is expressed in the Father's words: "the sweetest mother, Mary, of my only begotten Son. To her, out of reverence for the Word, is given this by my goodness: that anyone, whether just or sinner, who has due reverence for her, will not be snatched or devoured by the infernal demon" (c. 139).

The Lord continues: "She is like bait placed by my goodness to catch creatures" (ibid). This phrase effectively describes the mission of maternal mercy in its entirety. In many cases of conversion, such as that of Niccolò di Tuldo, the "presence of Mary" (letter 273) is invoked.[80] Indeed, her maternal mediation consists entirely in giving Jesus to us, in accompanying us when we seek to find him again in the temple of our soul, as she did in Jerusalem, and in presenting us to him.[81] "Pray to her, therefore, that she may represent you and give you to sweet Jesus, her Son: and she will do it, like a sweet and benign mother, and mother of mercy" (letter 144). Her "doctrine" or teaching is entirely about guiding us to Jesus (see letter 104); this doctrine is written within Mary by the Word who, by incarnating himself in her womb, made her the first written Gospel of his doctrine of life. "O Mary, in you is written the Word, from which we have the doctrine of life. You are the table on which he gives us doctrine" (prayer 21/XV).

Mary also fulfills her mission like a mirror and exemplar of every virtue. For example, she exemplifies humility, charity and prudence demonstrated at the incarnation (ibid.). Above all virtues, humility is exalted for its value:

> The humility of Mary pleased [God] so much that he was constrained by his goodness to give the Word of his only-begotten Son to her; and she was that sweet Mary who gave him to us. (letter 38; see letter 174; prayer 21/XV)

The poverty of Mary at Bethlehem is another admirable virtue. Finally, her love of God and of souls, which inspires her detachment from the bonds of blood, as well as her possession of the holiest of affections, are esteemed by everyone.

CHAPTER FOUR

THE TREE OF CHARITY

Knowledge penetrates now to the interior of our innermost being, that which we are, recreated in grace in the blood. What is this life and the elements of its development? What is, or should be, its dynamics? Let us see what Catherine of Siena has to say. Regarding the spiritual life, she offers us two complex images: one is botanical (the tree of charity) and the other is architectural (the bridge). In this chapter we will look only at the former image; in the remaining chapters we will look at the latter.

The tree of charity is a parable and an allegory.[82] As a parable, it is presented as a vision which she had "at the beginning of her life" (c. 44). God is a tree whose roots are united with the earth (incarnation); the topmost part of the tree is in heaven. Whoever wants to reach God must climb over a hedge of thorns which encircles the tree and attaches itself to the trunk and go to the top where it finds "inestimable sweetness" (ibid). Unfortunately, many turn back for fear of the thorns and eat some chaff (the deceptive delights of the world) close to the tree but then are still hungry and eventually die. The parable aims at demonstrating that pain (trials, difficulties, and sufferings) is an indispensable element in reaching, via the "way of truth," to true happiness found only in God.

The allegory, mentioned in the marvelous letter 213 and developed in the *Dialogue* (see cc. 9-11), gives a pedagogical and figurative unity to her moral teaching, taking its cue from analogous images of things in life (the human person, the soul, the crucifix, the virtues, sin) so as to give a more ample explanation of the origin and development of the virtues. Other similar allegories, but less developed, are: the soul as a city (see c. 144ff), the Church as a vineyard (see cc. 23-24) or the three vineyards (see letter 321).

Let us now turn to the outline of the allegory of the tree of charity. "The soul is a tree, made for love and it cannot live without love" (c. 10; see letter 363). This tree rises from the low ground or valley of humility in which it spreads its roots, which are the affections and desires. The ground of humility is circumscribed by a complete circle that has neither beginning nor end, representing knowledge of self united with knowledge of God which is without beginning or end. The tree is nourished by humility and sends forth a branch that is discretion, a singular Catherinian virtue which helps charity in giving to everyone what they need (to praise God and acknowledge graces received; to have holy hatred of one's self and to despise one's nothingness;[83] to pray for our neighbors and to give them good example, advice, and help). Discretion also gives proper measure to every other virtue. The core of this tree is patience, the possession of which means that God is indeed in the soul and the soul in God. From its different branches the tree "sends forth fragrant flowers of virtue" and fruits of various flavors, the latter representing the corporal and spiritual works of mercy that mature with the help of discretion. Finally, in another place, Catherine adds the final stroke of the brush: "the very top of the tree represents the soul's affections which no one can see, where one is united with the infinite God through the affection of love" (letter 113).

There is a *contra*-image: the soul of the sinner, which is the tree of death planted on the mountain of pride and nurtured by self-love, with a core that is impatience and branches of indiscretion. Made rotten by the worm of conscience, it produces deadly fruit (see c. 31ff; c. 93).

The often repeated principle, "The soul is made of love and created for love…it cannot live without love" (letter 113) means that the principal occupation of the soul, from the beginning to the end of life, is love. There is nothing easier or more pleasant, as is said elsewhere (see c. 55), since God does not ask us for anything else but love and in heaven will reward us "according to the measure of love and not according to the measure of our work or time" (c. 165).

The Genesis of Charity

Without giving definitions, Catherine starts from the Pauline concept of charity being the fullness of the Law and therefore it has an essential and central function in the spiritual life. Here are some of the ways she describes it: "Charity is that sweet and holy bond that binds the creature to his Creator; it binds man to God, and God to man" (letter 7). Elsewhere: "What is charity? It is ineffable love that the soul draws from its Creator with all its affection and strength" (letter 113). In these two descriptions, among many given by Catherine (see letter 322), we note the theological character, the unitive tendency of both, and its derivation from God. There is a natural sub-stratum for supernatural virtue and it is that we are made by love: "The matter of which you are made is love," says Eternal Truth to Catherine, "because I have created you for love, but you cannot live without love" (c. 110).

Derivation from God's Love

We note the first origins of charity: it comes from God. "This charity is a fire that proceeds from me, which carries off the heart and mind" of the saints and servants of God (c. 84). It is an infused grace, like faith and hope, given at baptism (see c. 98). Not only its origin but also its substance is something divine, as if a communication and participation in the eternal love ("I am the fire and you are the sparks" letter 70), like a vestment of fire that the Holy Spirit communicates to us, coming to live in the soul (see letter 129).

But the psychological genesis of charity as a virtue we are conscious of and that works in us is something else. Catherine explains it to us in her own way. First of all, the will needs to hunger to love given the fact that the will does not love by imposition. And so, "love is not acquired if not with love" (letters 29, 304). He who wants love looks for it. Where? The will moves the light (faith and knowledge) to look for it. "Without the light you cannot find it" and can be mistaken (see letter 304). It is a matter of seeing the one who truly loves us because "love comes from seeing oneself loved" (letter 47). In fact, "it is the nature of love that when the creature sees it is loved, immediately it loves" (letter 29); and one can add, "we love to the extent that we see ourselves loved" (letter 47). As St. Thomas Aquinas says, "Homines propter hoc quod amantur amant" ("Human beings love because they are loved").[84] This principle—of love being born from seeing oneself loved—is not always verified in natural loves, which are often unjustified and blind, but it is always true of the love of God because God always precedes us in love and we cannot "love him with this first one" (letter 94), i.e., we cannot arrive at love of him if he had not loved us first.

Where is this love found?—asks Catherine; and invariably she responds—"In holy knowledge of ourselves; seeing ourselves loved [by God] even before we came to exist" and finding in ourselves "the blood that manifested the love that God has for us" (letter 304). This is how love is born from light.

"As soon as the soul has found and seen in itself so much goodness of the Creator" (letter 29) it is inevitably taken by God: "it immediately loves." Every abstract consideration on the supreme Good that is infinitely loveable is absorbed existentially here. The one who does not love but desires to love must watch and set himself "to see in God only love" (letter 122). "So you see that from love, with the light, one acquires love" (letter 29). The conclusion seems necessary; Catherine expresses in her logic that which she had certainly experienced: "And if man wants to serve and love God, the eye of the intellect opens, focusing on its object; and love attracts love: that is, seeing that God supremely loves him, he cannot but love him" (letter 122).

From knowledge is born love. To comprehend the legitimacy of this connection, *quasi* necessary, between knowledge and love we must note that Catherine speaks "in general," that is of what happens in and of itself apart from whatever can disturb the knowledge of individual persons. The principle remains: from knowledge is born love. It is understood that from imperfect knowledge will come imperfect love or no love at all. Here Catherine is correct: "We love as much as we know, and we know as much as we see; the more the light is perfect, the more perfectly we see" (letter 343). Regarding this, Catherine always notes that first of all we must make sure that our visual faculty, the intellect, is clear so as to free us from "self-love, which is a cloud that does not let us know and see the truth of that which we must love" (letter

304). This signifies a condition that is not purely intellectual but moral; that is, it takes a humble search of love, free from the clouds of self-love, "this perfect knowledge and, with knowledge, love" (letter 47).

Therefore, having cleared the way, one can say that in itself and on equal terms "the one who knows more, loves more" (c. 131) and that every exception would confirm the rule. It is almost proportional: "As much as you open the eye of the intellect to see the fire and the abyss of God's inestimable love towards you...to that extent you will be constrained to love him in truth" (letter 47). At this point it is necessary to have faith and to meditate. To Catherine's pure soul, it seems impossible that this shouldn't always happen, and she often says: "Seeing so much love, how can you not love?" (letter 96). "So...one should not hold back the will, and I don't know how it could be held back, and not run...to love that which God loves" (letter 181). "I cannot think of anyone who does not love after seeing himself so much loved, unless he obscures the light with his self-love" (letter 177; see letters 188, 200, 297, etc.).

Charity is born through contact. A further search, at a deeper level, makes us understand that we receive God's charity not in a pure intellectual way but by contact with him or by transmission by others. This is what Catherine teaches about every supernatural and Christian virtue, whereas for her every natural virtue is imperfect or dead because it does not bring one to eternal life.[85] For the specifically Christian character of charity and of every virtue, the underlying principle is: "Every virtue has in itself life through Christ crucified...insofar as the soul has drawn love from him" (c. 4) and "No one can have virtue that gives the life of grace if it is not from him" (c. 27).

Regarding the character of divine virtue, we note that the supernatural origin of charity is not initially found in our deliberate contact with God but rather in the fact that, having found in ourselves the love that God has for us, it spreads rapidly like fire and produces in us the *"fuoco d'amore"* or fire of love. It is not a movement that begins on our part with an act that leads to its realization. That would be illogical, Catherine explains, because knowledge does not proceed alone but opens the way for affection, symbolized by the topmost part of the tree ("the top, that is the soul's affection, that goes directly to the intellect"). Affection, having discovered living love because of God's presence in us, brings about in us through love the creation and regeneration of grace: "So affection is united with the affection of Christ crucified, and with love draws to itself love" (letter 113).[86] An image illustrates this fact: "Our heart, when it is enamored by divine love, is like a sponge that draws water to itself." Everything is for the purpose of uniting the two things: the heart and the "fire of divine charity." So, as has been said: "From love and with love we attract love" (letter 113). This way of drawing or eliciting virtue from God, charity in particular, is expressed in Catherine's often repeated saying that we will find it in the open side of Christ (see letter 318, etc.), as we will see in a moment.

It seems that virtual or efficient contact with God is produced—although we do not know at what point—by prayer, which "unites the soul to God" (letter 67; c. 1), i.e., it accomplishes on the level of the real and affective that which the light did on the intellectual level. This is a principle which has an Aristotelian-scholastic flavor that is valid for every virtue: "The more we come to God, the more we participate in his goodness and sense the odor of virtue; because only he is the teacher of the virtues and in him we receive them; and prayer is what unites us with the supreme Good" (letter 203).

In conclusion, this richness of images is to make us understand that charity is derived from the love that is God, "a love that the soul draws from its Creator," a response to the love that God has for us.

Love of Neighbor

Love of neighbor is not an additional virtue with origins in something other than the love of God. It is the same charity, so to speak, executed in action externally although charity may have its own acts directed to God (affection, praise, holy desire, union, tasting God's presence). Love of neighbor is proof that God is operating in the soul and that the soul wants to reciprocate the love that God shows it.

Three fundamental principles serve to introduce this transfer of the object loved. First, the duty of being useful to our neighbor since we cannot be such for God (see c. 7; letters 8, 50, 51, 94, 103, 113, 151, 203, 226, 254, etc.). We are in debt to God who has loved us. We are in the debt of love and love must be proved by deeds, otherwise it is not true love. But what can we do for God who does not need anything or anyone? The Lord says: "Since you cannot do anything for me, you must do it for your neighbor" (c.7). Charity authorizes this exchange since it is nothing other than "loving what God loves" (letters 8, 181); in fact, according to the normal criteria, "it is the nature of love to love all those things that are loved by the beloved" (letter 51; see letter 279). It is therefore natural to turn our attention to the neighbor for the love of God, knowing that "God supremely loves him" (letters 51, 226), as has been shown with the blood shed not only for us but for our neighbor. "Love him...because he is loved by me" (c. 89).

Second, we love our neighbor because God distributes his gifts in various ways so as to give everyone the opportunity to help others. He wanted that "one would have need of the other" because all would be forced by necessity to "practice charity one for the other." For this reason he has distributed his gifts, psychological and moral, in such a way that no one may have all of them in the grade of perfection (c. 7; see c. 148).

Third, "every virtue is exercised by means of our neighbor, as well as every defect" (c. 6). This principle, repeated many times (see c. 89; letters 104, 151, etc.) does not minimize the question of the difference of the various virtues but strongly underscores the grave social dimension of every human act, good or evil, however hidden or personal it may be. The principle gives to the charity of God an indispensable and unlimited dimension, which few of the Protestant commentators are aware of. Catherine frequently speaks of it in different ways: "in God we conceive the virtues, and we give birth to them in our neighbor" (letters 50, 104); "give honor to God and hard work to one's neighbor" (letters 104, 164, etc.).

Catherine's thought on this is seen in her teaching that whatever may be done, good or bad, is done to oneself or to others, and is good or bad for the entire world because of the law of universal solidarity or of the communion of saints (or of "general assistance that must be done for every creature," c. 6). In fact, whatever is done gives us, takes away from us, or diminishes the charity of God in us without which nothing supernaturally virtuous or positive can be accomplished. Whatever is done without charity is never irrelevant to our neighbor because it is detrimental to oneself "who is one's principal neighbor" (c. 6), or is detrimental to one's neighbor because of our evil or unjust actions, or that which would have been only virtuous on the natural order is now deprived of supernatural value and merit to the detriment of oneself and others. From here we can deduce several corollaries:

- "Love of virtue is tested and fortified by means of our neighbor" (letter 151; see letter 104);
- "With the [same] perfection with which we love God, we love also the rational creature" (letter 263; see c. 7, etc.);
- "There is no other way to attain virtue except by means of love of neighbor" (letter 104).
- "There is nothing good [says Eternal Truth] that can be done except in charity for me and for your neighbor, and if it is not done in this charity it cannot be anything good, and cannot be a true good, even if one's actions may be virtuous" (c. 145).

The loneliness of the soul without charity: "You do not want the soul to be alone without love of you and neighbor. The soul is then perfectly united when it is thus accompanied.... But when the soul is accompanied by sin [colpa], it remains alone, because it has left you who are all good. Being apart from you, it is separated also from love of neighbor and is accompanied with sin, which is nothing" (prayer19/XXII).

This "means" by which we love God, that is the neighbor, is equally implicated, directly or indirectly,[87] in every evil act because self-love, having brought about the loss of charity, opens the door to every sin against love of neighbor (see cc. 6-8). In this way no one is saved or damned without the neighbor. The same teaching, animated by a modern apostolic sense, is found in the allegory of the three vineyards where it is said that some benefit cannot be done to the vineyard of our own soul that is not also done to the vineyard of our neighbor's soul (see letter 321).

This, then, is how that which is called the descent and ascent of love is completed. In the descending line love comes from God to us and from us it is extended to the neighbor in the exercise of every virtue. In the ascending line, all the virtues and good works, lived out in one's love of neighbor, prove that love of God is actually in the soul and, being an exchange of affection, carry the soul ever closer to God.

Vital Connection of the Virtues to Charity

All that has been said now brings us to consider the preeminent place of charity in the fabric of Christian virtues.[88] The primacy of love in Christian life immediately emerges. In it consists every obligation and virtue, so much so that Catherine says: "All that I ask of you is charity" (c. 55). Charity is the most perfect and indispensable virtue because it alone unites us to God (see letter 97), "gives the life of grace" to the soul (letter 113) and, as we have seen, makes it to participate in the blood and the fire. In addition, it is the most perfect virtue because charity gives "life to every virtue" such that "no virtue can have it [=life] without charity" (c. 7). Last of all, charity is the most perfect because it alone enters heaven while it is only the fruits of the other virtues that do so; in fact, in heaven we "need only charity, which is love, because eternal life is nothing other than love, with which we can taste the essence of God. His love has made us worthy to see him face to face, the sight of whom is our beatitude" (letter 345).

In particular, charity is the "mother of all virtues" in a way entirely proper and complete, i.e., from the formal point of view of specifically Christian virtue: interior forces that make it possible for us to accomplish inspired works of love of God worthy of eternal life, "The truth gives us light, and with the light leads us to the gate of life eternal" (letter 345). The allegory of the tree illustrates it: "all the virtues are bound together in charity" (c. 7) like branches to a tree from which they receive the one and only sap that produces flowers and flavorful fruits. In a specific way, charity is the "mother of all virtues" inasmuch as it alone gives the other virtues contact with the wellspring of all virtues that is God himself (see letter 203), being built into the walls of the Christ-Bridge or grafted onto Christ (see c. 27).

Charity "is a mother who conceives in the soul her children, the virtues, and gives birth to them for the honor of God in [our relationship with] one's neighbor" (letter 33). The concept is repeated often (see cc. 11, 61, 74, etc.), insisting in a special way that "she brings to birth children, the virtues, who are alive and not dead" (letters 32, 97), meaning that charity brings about the birth of the other virtues by giving them the inspiration and the motive of charity "for love of God" and also in ordering to eternal life the works of the other virtues. It is like making them go out (after being born) from the "intrinsic virtue" of the soul so as to pass on to the neighbor the good actions done for the glory of God (see c. 74).

Concretely speaking, how do we see this connection of the virtues and how they are intertwined? Catherine's visual allegories illustrate the preceding affirmations. First of all, we note that it is a vital connection, one that affects life, and therefore Catherine expresses it with figurative language: the tree with flowers and fruits, the mother who gives birth and then nurses, etc. In addition, she is not speaking of dead virtue (virtues of a quality that is natural and good, but without sanctifying grace and supernatural inspiration), but of living virtue, meriting eternal life (see letters 32, 97, 304). The fabric of the virtues, although under the command of charity, is realized by a reciprocal connection which draws upon each virtue, so that a person "cannot have just one of the virtues out of all of them because all are linked together" (c. 7). The typical example is that of the three theological virtues: "Of these virtues, one stands behind the other; loves does not exist without faith, nor faith without love. These are three columns that hold up the rock of our soul" (letter 69). In the description of the tree of charity that flourishes in an encircled garden of knowledge, the principal Catherinian virtues begin to grow in this way:

- The earth or ground represents *humility* in which the roots sink and are nourished by charity which "nurses and feeds" humility, "the little virtue";
- The tree is *charity;*
- On the side of the tree is the shoot of *discretion*;
- In the core of the tree trunk is *patience,* "the queen of the virtues," of which Catherine often sings its praises (see cc. 77, 95; letters 104, 355, etc.), assigning to it the function of an infallible sign that demonstrates or guarantees the actual existence in the soul of charity and the other virtues (see c. 1; letter 39);
- On the tree grow branches and fragrant flowers that are all *the other virtues* from which come the fruits of every good work (see cc. 9-11; letter 213).

The Struggle of the Virtues Against the Vices

Regarding each of the virtues already mentioned, and of the others we have not mentioned such as obedience, perseverance, fortitude, gratitude, etc., Catherine speaks about each, their development and perfection, individually according to the occasion, as we will see. However, she never ceases talking about the struggle of the virtues to survive since she conceives of the spiritual life as a battle which is dominated by the cross, marked by the blood, nourished by suffering lovingly embraced and decidedly masculine: "and the blood has remained on the battle field to give life to us knights, so as to fight manfully without any fear" (letter 114).[89] Life is full of adversaries. Christ and the devil invite us in opposite directions (see letter 318), one to the living water and the other to the water of death (see c. 53); one to truth, the other to falsehood (see c. 42). Charity, "mother and nurse of all virtues" (letter 279) has as its opponent self-love, the "principle and foundation of every evil" (c. 7). The light of faith has as its opponent the darkness of sin. Even virtue is never secure if it has not been tested by its contrary (see cc. 8, 43; letters 71, 211); and love of virtue is not genuine if it is not allied with hatred of vice (see c. 65). So, the life of the soul advances always in a state of battle from which we cannot absent ourselves because it is always happening within us, and because in it we achieve the securest earnings of all: winning a virtue that has been tested (see letters 62, 71).

There are other traditional enemies of ours—the world, the devil, the flesh (see letters 114, 197, 345)—but the one that we fight against most is self-love, which is within us and for that reason is the most dangerous (see letter 315), as we have already seen and will see, being allied to the "perverse law" of the senses (see c. 96).

On our side there are our friends and aids. The blood animates us for battle through the memory (see letter 245), unites us with the supreme fortitude that is God (see letter 195), fortifies the rock that is the soul's faculty of the will (see letter 36), and imparts the energy of grace so that we will not be intimidated by any enemy (see c. 14; letters 331, 332, etc.). When our will is fortified by the blood it is united to the will of God: "the will has such fortitude that neither the devil nor any creature can ever weaken it if ones does not want it" (letter 245). Prayer, the indispensable armor in defending oneself against every adversary (see c. 65), is to be strong and persevering (see letter 154) so as to win every battle (see letter 315).

The qualities required to win, according to Catherine, are above all an *absolute determination,* in no uncertain terms, without postponements or delays: "Do not let pass the least thought outside of God that is not corrected with great reproach" (letter 265; see letters 21, 315, 321, 361, etc.; cc. 60, 73). The *watch dog of conscience,* nourished by the blood (see letter 114), who barks at every enemy, must be kept awake. Another important quality is *manly cour-*

age, to the point of "blood for blood" if necessary (letter 143), which is not weak or childish: "Do not be a frightened child, be a man" (letter 239 to the Pope; see letter 206). Charity found to the degree that "we will be manly because the feminine will that makes us fainthearted has been extinguished" (letter 245). Also necessary is *perseverance* (see c. 52) without ever looking away from the direction in which we are plowing (c. 12 and passim), with *patience and fortitude* that never leaves one disheartened (see letter 150). Last of all, an unfailing *optimism* that comes from faith in God's eternal love and from confidence in the power of his blood that has defeated all our enemies:

> [He] came like our captain, with an unarmed hand, nailed and fastened to the cross, having defeated our enemies…. The devil becomes powerless through the blood of this Lamb…. The flesh is defeated by the lashes and torments of Christ, and the world with its opprobrium, scorn, insults and abuse. (letter 114).

Prayer in the Development and Defense of the Virtues

We have already mentioned several times *orazione*—as Catherine ordinarily calls prayer (*preghiera*).[90] We will now speak about it more specifically, even though briefly, because in the panorama of the virtues it is an essential energy for the tree of charity. What is it? For Catherine, it is a movement of the soul, moved by the Holy Spirit, founded on knowledge and with the purpose of uniting us with God. The elements of this description are taken from different parts of the Catherinian corpus because no definitions are given. Prayer is a raising of the mind (see c. 66), an act of our spirit, and therefore a movement of the soul. It is inspired and impelled by the Spirit of God (see cc. 4, 86; letters 28, 86) dwelling in the soul; it is in fact the Spirit who makes us pray, not our devices. This is the clearest proof that he wants to hear our prayers, otherwise he would not move us (see letter 266). Prayer is founded on the knowledge of oneself (i.e., on the humble recognition of one's poverty and need before God) and on the knowledge of God's goodness "who knows, is able and wants to answer our just petitions" (letter 325). This is the same as saying that prayer is founded on humility and charity (see letter 154). Prayer means to encounter God (see letter 81) and be united to him in desire and love (see c. 1; letters 67, 358, etc.).

Its progressive forms, rising from the most imperfect, are vocal prayer, mental prayer, and continuous prayer. Vocal prayer consists in the recitation of prayers already made: this is the least perfect (see letters 26, 150, 353), but prayer must always start from here if one wants to reach the most perform form (see c. 66). Mental prayer is entirely internal, of thought and sentiment, when the soul "with an angelic mind, is united to God through the affection of love and with the light of the intellect sees and understands, and clothes itself in truth" (letter 26). Continuous prayer is habitual (the other two are made in the present moment) consisting in the continuous disposition of the soul, in which desire and affection are extended and transferred to the performance of external activity (c. 66).[91] Catherinian characteristics of this type of prayer are indicated in different ways: "continuous prayer of holy desire"; "affection of charity is continuous prayer"; "prayer of the good and holy will"; "prayer as charity for one's neighbor"; "he who does not cease to pray does not cease to do good," taken from a gloss from Cavalca (see c. 66; letter 351; see letters 22, 26, 154, 353, etc).[92]

On the necessity of prayer, Catherine gives us two considerations that she refers to frequently and which pertain first to the birth and then to the defense of the virtues. Prayer is "the mother of the virtues" but in a different sense from charity: "Straight away this prayer is a mother who out of love of God conceives the virtues and out of love of neighbor gives birth to them" (letter 26); i.e., prayer, inspired and guided by charity, accompanies the whole formation process in the solidification and exercise of every virtue (see c. 66). Charity produces all the virtues in both a generic and specific sense. Prayer, on the other hand, does it in subordination to charity, through meditation in asking for and obtaining the virtues from God, the teacher and wellspring of all virtues (see letter 203), and in bringing about the virtues, as we have seen, through effective contact with God (see letter 81).

Prayer is a spiritual weapon, i.e., a means of entreating God, and its strength comes particularly from the fact of conforming oneself to the "desire" of God, for inasmuch as one conquers vice and receives virtue one is conformed: "The soul receives and tastes to one degree of perfection or another this mother, prayer, inasmuch as it feeds on the angelic food of God's holy desire" (letter 353). Prayer's strength also comes from trusting with complete confidence on one's faith in the redemptive value of the blood: "Prayer is a mother clothed with fire and inebriated by blood" (letter 150).

Prayer is a weapon "with which the soul defends itself from every adversary" (c. 65) and which must never be put down or given away (see letters 36, 56, 71, 335), or it will happen to us what happened to the Israelites who battled and won when Moses held up the staff of God and lost when it was lowered (see letter 315; Ex 17:11). It is also a weapon insofar as it is the unique and indispensable means to obtain what we lack from God, who knows, is able, and also wants to give us much more than we ask (see letters 196, 353).

The qualities of genuine prayer are summarized by Catherine in three adjectives: humble, continuous, and faithful:

Humble, I say; drawn from the knowledge of oneself, seeing that of ourselves we have no being except inasmuch as we are made and created by God. Continuous, I say, drawn from the knowledge of the goodness of God in oneself, where we have seen that God is continuously at work in us, pouring out over us many graces and blessings. And I say faithful, for prayer hopes in truth, and with firm and living faith believes that God knows, can and wants to answer our just petitions and give us those things necessary for our salvation. (letter 325; see letters 81, 213; *Dialogue,* passim)

CHAPTER FIVE

THE CHRIST-BRIDGE: *FIRST STAIR*

The Allegory of the Bridge

Let us begin by examining the development of the allegory of the bridge. From some biblical-liturgical metaphors concerning the cross (as a tree, cathedra, ladder) matured the figure of the bridge that is presented in allegorical form in a vision narrated by Catherine in letter 272. It is difficult to assign to the allegory a literary source or recollection of a specific piece of architecture she might have known of or seen. For it to develop from just a visual image into a figure of a living process, and from just a symbol or theoretical schema to a practical interpretation of the soul's journey towards heaven, traditional elements of asceticism and the Catherinian charismatic sense concerning the mystery of salvation converged. Particularly the Gospel phrases, "I am the way" (Jn 14:6) and "When I am lifted up from the earth, I will draw all people to myself" (Jn 12:32), together with a line from Domenico Cavalca (†1342), "The heart of man cannot be attracted by any other way but by love,"[93] besides the traditional division of the spiritual life into three states, have all contributed to a building up of this spiritual way of passage.

As a universal description of what happens to the soul journeying towards its goal, an historical-ideological outline develops that is closer to the Dante's *Divine Comedy* than to the *Ascent of Mount Carmel* by St. John of the Cross, but it is less autobiographical than Dante and does not fit easily into any systematic classification and is more christological than the sanjuanist theory.

Two facts presuppose the bridge: original sin and the incarnation. The road to heaven "was broken by Adam's sin and disobedience," in the sense that no good work was sufficient to bring someone to eternal life; heaven and the gates of divine mercy were closed. "No sooner had Adam sinned than a tempestuous river started flowing" in the ravine separating God and humanity which swept away everything and prevented everyone from reaching the blessed shore. "The river is nothing other than the darksome sea of this darksome life" (c. 21; see letter 272). To remedy all these evils, the Eternal Father sent his Son to earth to be our mediator and to re-open the gates of heaven with his cross and with his blood.

The bridge goes from earth to heaven because it is Christ in whom the divine nature is united to the human nature; with his doctrine and his grace he is the way for us to eternal life. The stones of which the bridge is made are "the true and real virtues," living stones inserted in Christ. The bridge has only one span but above it is a staircase with three ascending stairs that Catherine calls *scaloni* in her Sienese dialect. Since the bridge is Christ, the stairs are marked on his body (like projections of rock that allow a mountain climber to stop and rest) in his wounded feet, in his side, and in the mouth (see c. 26). Whoever wants to ascend to heaven must pass through these stages either in a general way by a concentration of the soul's three powers or in a particular way in accordance with the perfection of love.[94] He who stays in the river or returns to it is drowned, swept away by the stormy river which represents the corruption of sin and the deceit of the world.

To support the wayfarers who climb the staircase, a storeroom is placed on the bridge where they are refreshed: this is the Church that "administers the bread of life and gives the draft of blood" (c. 27), that is, administers the sacraments, especially the Eucharist. The one who goes on the bridge, responding to Christ's invitation that he is Truth, follows "the way of truth" that leads one to true salvation. The one who travels in the river under the bridge, accepting the invitation of the devil who is the father of lies, follows the "way of falsehood" and is carried away in the ever-changing and deceiving current of the world which ends in damnation (see cc. 27, 42, etc.; letter 318). Regarding the characteristics of the spiritual theory of the bridge, we mention only some of them now:

- It follows the triple division of the degrees of the spiritual life (purgative, illuminative, unitive).
- It applies to everyone who strives toward "the great perfection."
- Progress is presented in a vertical perspective.
- Perfection hinges on the progressive evolution of charity.
- Perfection is the result of the normal development of the spiritual life.
- The critical passages from one stage to another depend upon the dialectic of knowledge and self-love, which are antithetically opposed.

We will follow the theory of the bridge-staircase as found in the *Dialogue*, supplementing it with corresponding elements which pertain to it from Catherine's other writings. This theory is the *rule* of the spiritual journey as shown to Catherine by the Divine Master:

> This was the rule that he taught once to one of his servants [=Catherine], saying: "Get up, daughter, rise above yourself, and climb on me. And so that you can climb up, I made for you the staircase which is nailed to the cross." (letter 74; see letters 75, 120, 34)

Out of the River

To save oneself from the tempestuous river of the world and of sin, the soul must come out of it, flinging oneself on the shore.

This first movement takes place by the convergence of three elements. First, there is the *crisis of knowledge.* Sinners come to realize that they are heading toward perdition, that they are being deceived by the world and by the father of lies, to become "martyrs of the devil," because by believing in him they shall receive nothing but damnation, meanwhile they now see that, all things considered, "in this life the just have a better destiny than sinners" (c. 48).

Second, there is *servile fear,* i.e., the fear of unhappiness in this life and of punishments in the life to come, with disgust of the world and boredom with oneself (see c. 49). While it is true that this servile fear is normally an impulse towards the "first change" or conversion, if the soul remains only in the fear of punishment it will not persevere and be saved. As a matter of fact, this fear can be overcome by passing through the momentary prosperities of life or through the horror of adversities, persecutions and spiritual battles, which the just must confront in life (ibid.). It requires a positive reason to stabilize the conversion; love must be united with fear, filling the house, which has been swept clean of fear, with the "virtues founded on love" (ibid.), that is to say not only freed from evil but free to will and do the good.[95] Fear is also not enough because we are now under the new law, i.e., the law of love given us by the Son of God (see c.58). The soul, therefore, moved by knowledge of self and of God and illuminated by faith, begins to detest sin not so much because of fear of punishment but out of fear of offending God: this is a first glimmer of love contained in the "holy fear" of God (see cc. 58-59).

Third, there is *penance and confession.* To leave the river and vomit the corrupt water is the sign that concludes this change (see c. 49) and signifies a living repentance of faults and a complete confession, caused by an impulse given by "a pang of conscience" (c. 94).

Tears

In the spiritual life not one important step happens without tears (see c. 87), because the heart feels every detachment and every gain realized by the soul and it is expressed more-or-less with tears that are visible.[96] Therefore, different changes correspond to different types of tears. The tears, then, become signs of the states of the soul and so also of the spiritual states. Put in proper order, they indicate the journey of the soul along an original schema that is Catherine's own. There are five kinds of tears, rising from the least to the most perfect (see c. 88):

- the tears of worldly persons who are being drawn to desperation and damnation;

- tears of servile love;
- tears of compassion of the imperfect;
- tears of sweetness of the perfect;
- tears of love of the most perfect, which are often followed by what Catherine calls "tears of fire" that are totally interior.

With the exception of the first kind of tears, which are "tears of death," all the others are "tears of life" because they alone confer spiritual life.

Catherine delivers a long and bitter analysis of the tears of death shed by sinners who are carried away by the river (see cc. 93-94),[97] in the course of which she describes the four winds (prosperity, adversity, servile fear, and remorse) that shake them up and ready them for their destruction.

The first tears of life, the tears of compassion of the imperfect, are shed by those "who have started to overcome faults through fear of punishment" (c. 95); they come out of the river and "for fear of punishment began to weep" (c. 89). It is the weeping characteristic of this passage from the death of sin to the life of grace. Having taken the first step, the soul climbs to the first stair of the bridge and, freed from the tension of fear, is drawn by the sensation of a secure place, by the attraction and taste of a new state with the joys of redis-covered innocence. If the soul passes from servile fear to holy fear of God, it begins to shed tears of consolation that contribute to its passage to the second stair and are already better than the preceding tears but nevertheless are im-perfect because they still have much that is sensual and are shed, above all, out of compassion for oneself (see cc. 89, 95).

Invitation to Climb

The Law of Progress

The soul that is away from the open waters seems to discover only now that highest Bridge, who invites it to climb up. If it understands the invitation and responds, it enters into the logic of the ascent, commanded by the knowledge and love that attract it and push it on to the gate of heaven; other-wise, it falls back into the river.

Christ invites and attracts the soul towards the living water, while the dev-il attracts the soul to the water of death (see cc. 42-44; letter 318). Christ, however, attracts with a particular attraction ("When I am lifted up from the earth, I will draw everyone to me": Jn 12:32) by means of love, which is ac-cording to human nature which is attracted above all by love ("Trahit sua quemque voluptas"—each man is led by his own taste, according to an old Roman saying). Be careful: Jesus calls only those who are thirsty: "Let any-one who is thirsty come to me…and drink" (Jn 7:37, 38). "He does not invite those who are not thirsty," notes Catherine (letter 318); in fact, only those who are thirsty feel the call of the fount of Life, although we are "all invited generally and particularly" (c. 53). Therefore, to accept the invitation and go to the fount the soul must be "thirsty and hungry for virtue" (letter 164). He who wants to find charity must first be willing to love.

First of all, the *law of progress* asserts itself: "The soul that does not make the first change cannot proceed; therefore, if it does not go forward it turns backward" (c. 49; see c. 99; letter 290). We are reminded of the ancient saying: "non progredi est regredi" (not to go forward is to go backward).

Second, *the soul rises through stages that are ordered and progressive*: "the bridge has three stairs, so that, climbing the first and the second, you can reach the last" (c. 26). Catherine is not fanatical about a system; she is just convinced that the life of grace can not be disordered and flat; and that the line of spiritual development goes from the least to the most perfect (see c. 60). Besides, God normally does not lead us to the stages of perfection if we are not yet prepared in ourselves, as expressed in the saying: "God loves us as we love him" (letter 94; c. 60).

Universal Call [98]

The invitation is extended to each and every human being (see c. 53; letter 215) and is a call to charity. Charity is of two kinds: *common charity* is the actual (=in fact) observance of the commandments and only the "mental" observance of the evangelical counsels (that is, through desire, intention, and in spirit (see cc. 47, 53, 56; letter 215, etc.).[99] *Perfect charity* consists in the actual observance not only of the commandments but also the counsels (ibid.); these are the generous souls, particularly the religious who for this reason abandon the world and observe the three vows. The difference is entirely in the "mental or actual" counsels (see c. 53), i.e., whether they are observed only in the soul's interior disposition or in actual fact. However, the actual observance is not only material (to act well only because there is no occasion to act badly) but it is also mental, i.e., with the soul disposed under no circumstances to do evil. In this sense marital continence is also observed. Thus we need the mental observance of the counsels in the exercise of common charity if it is to be true charity, i.e., to live according to the will of God and with an orderly love of earthly things (see c.47). It is in this sense that Catherine says: "the counsels are tied to the commandments: no one can observe the commandments who does not observe the counsels, not in actual fact but mentally" (ibid.).

The two states of life—the common and the perfect—are both good and lead to salvation, because God is not "a respecter of states [of life] but of holy desires" (c. 47)[100] and rewards "according to the measure of love and not according to one's work or time" (c. 145). The second state, however, is more pleasing to God because souls seek the "great perfection" (ibid.) and "are made angels" in the observance of their state (letter 215).

The common state is more general and is obligatory, and possible, for everyone: "This is the way that everyone must keep to in whatever state a person may be...; every creature can do it, must do it and is obliged to do it" (c. 55), no condition in life can make it impossible provided one lives "with a good and holy will," i.e., with the love of God expressed in fidelity to his law without being enslaved by others. Placed as it must be on the plane of love, this common state is possible for everyone:

It is an easy thing, because nothing is as easy and delightful as love. Now, that which I ask of you is nothing other than love and predilection of me and of neighbor. This can be done at any time, in any place and in every state of life, loving and keeping everything for the praise and glory of my name. (c. 55)

General Stairs

What does it mean for one who is in common charity to climb the bridge? There are two ways to consider the stairs of the bridge: the general stairs (*scaloni generali*) for the common state and the particular stairs (*scaloni particolari*) for those seeking the great perfection in perfect charity. We will first examine the former.

The general stairs represent the doctrine of Christ lived in substantial fidelity to the commandment of love of God and neighbor by way of the simultaneous participation of the soul's three powers: *memory* which is full of the blessings of God, *intellect* that meditates on the warm-hearted love shown us by the incarnate Son, and the *will* that loves the divine goodness (see c. 54). This is the joining together or "gathering together of the three powers" in the name of God, which fulfills the words of Christ: "Where two or three are gathered in my name, I am there among them" (Mt 18:20). Once the soul's powers are gathered together in charity, God is in the soul with "the company of many virtues" (c. 54) joined with charity.

At this point the three stairs, symbolized in the soul's three powers, come into operation because the simultaneous exercise of the powers, constantly repeated and maintained with living faith, is like a recurrence of the first gathering together of the three (see c. 59) and results in a continuous and secure advance:

Once the two are gathered together, namely love of me and of neighbor, and the memory gathers together to hold, and the intellect to see and the will to love, the soul finds itself accompanied by me who is its strength and security; it discovers the company of the virtues, and it goes forward and remains secure because I am in the midst of them. (c. 54)

The creature is on the bridge; if it glimpses, albeit indistinctly, the ascent with an ever more perfect engagement of the soul's three spiritual faculties, without servile fear, and thirsts for living water, following the doctrine of Christ, i.e., the bridge, the faculties free themselves from the attraction of transitory things through holy fear of God; they immerse themselves in reason's search for the warm-hearted love of Christ; they fill themselves with love and find peace by quenching their thirst at the "fount of living water," passing through the gate that is Christ crucified (see cc. 54-55).

On the First Stair

At the Feet of the Crucified

The soul puts its feet on the first stair when it begins to overcome servile fear; from being shipwrecked, one now becomes a wayfarer and pilgrim. Immediately it finds itself at the feet of the Crucified: this is the level of the first stair or spiritual stage. Underneath it flows the river which cannot harm it because the soul is at a higher place. Moreover, in Christ "there was none of the venom of sin" (c. 26). It is here that the soul, following the example of Christ, lifts its feet from the earth, rids itself of vice, and feels the attraction of love that comes from the Crucified (see c. 26). Let us examine more closely each.

To detach the feet from the earth is indispensable for putting oneself at a safe distance from the dangers of the river, from fear of the spell of sin; it does not mean to isolate oneself from the world but to be detached from its affections (which are two, like our two feet: love and desire; see c. 49). The affections are for the soul like its feet by which it can advance in any direction (see c. 26), according to an often repeated phrase of St. Augustine: *"Non movetur anima pedibus sed affectibus"* ("The soul does not walk on feet but on affections").[101] This function of detachment is also assigned the first place in Catherine's dying words or her "Spiritual Testament."[102]   At this point it is sensuality, above all, that is targeted, the part of ourselves closest to the earth; it must be "trampled with the feet of affection" (letter 62). Since the feet of Jesus are "nailed to the cross," so also must the disordered affections be crucified, "stripping them of every disordered will that does not seek or want anything other than Christ crucified...; desiring to bear every undeserved pain, both bodily pain and mental pain" (letter 309).

To strip oneself of vice is characteristic of this first stair, as clothing oneself in virtue and the taste of peace are characteristic of the second and third stairs (see c. 26). There is no need to speak again about the war between the virtues and the vices, which more than any other activity at this point begins here by imposing on the soul the final choice between the unhappiness of vice and the joy of virtue (see cc. 28, 31-40), taking hold of the knife of love of virtue and hatred of vice (see c. 36), since it is clear that the way of vice is the river's current that carries one off to damnation and is the pledge of hell (see cc. 45-46). It is not only a matter of freeing oneself from a specific fault in confession but of being set free from enslavement to the habitual disposition to evil, from the fascination of its deceitful pleasure, in other words from the attachment to disordered pleasures, otherwise we will never succeed in putting both feet on the first stair (see c. 49) and the intellect will always be blinded by self-love (see c. 46).

At the root of everything is the "venom of our own sensuality" (c. 47), this "perverse law which always assails the spirit" (c. 51) and which must be a servant and not a master.[103] Therefore, "we must first strip the soul's affections of all self-will" (letter 75); but this is not accomplished until we are led to "kill this perverse sensitive will" by courageously cutting off every manifestation of a tendency toward vice (see letter 265).[104] Catherine persistently reminds us of this purifying work, so much more striking at this point that it is usually called the purgative way, by showing the soul's intellect the harm that comes from sensitive self-love which transforms our tree of life into a tree of death "which does not produce anything else but the fruit of death, putrid flowers, blotched leaves," etc., (c. 93).

The attraction of love is absolutely decisive, even though it does not seem dominant in this apparently negative phase but is actually growing. If we ask ourselves why the bridge is "raised on high," Catherine hears the answer from the Eternal Father that the Son of God climbed the cross to give us the greatest demonstration of love and to *attract us* with his love. Thus, Christ said: "If I am lifted up I will draw all things to myself" (c. 26; see Jn 12:32). In accordance with what was said earlier on the genesis of charity, love attracts love. Taking the concept and the expression from Cavalca,[105] Catherine puts forward the principle that dominates the entire dynamic of the bridge: "The heart of man is always attracted by love" (c. 26); therefore, in light of Jn 12:32, once the heart of an individual is attracted the whole person is attracted with all the powers of one's soul and in all one's dimensions, according to the exegesis of St. Gregory the Great that Catherine makes her own: "The whole man is drawn, everything else is drawn with him, because everything is made for him" (c. 26).[106]

Catherine has the genius to apply this universal attraction on the line of love to her entire theory and to every level of the spiritual life. On this dynamic of the allegory, the cross is transformed into a living bridge and a staircase that brings us up high to heaven. This means that if the soul at the very beginning is not attracted by a minimum of Christ's love, it will never have the strength to climb the bridge of salvation. To look at Christ and his life is the only way to encourage oneself to leave behind the corruption of sin and rise above the attraction of the world. The Eternal Truth says expressly this:

"There would be no other remedy [=to prevent] its falling back into the river" (c.58). Moreover, there is a void that must be filled completely by love. The soul, created for love, cannot bear this emptiness; therefore, having swept the heart clean of all the disordered affections of the world, if it is thirsty for living water (that is, for a love that is not a lie) immediately it begins and fills itself of heavenly love with the water of grace that is found once again (see c. 54; see letters 263, 272).

Mercenary Love and the Servile State

This is the condition of those who are on the first stair. Love is as necessary for the human person as food (see cc. 10, 51, 93; letter 263); and so it is logical that here also we find a certain kind of love. But the love that someone is able to express at this point is imperfect: it is the love of a mercenary servant (see cc. 56, 60), of a person who serves for payment and out of fear of losing it. It is pointless to deceive ourselves of being immediately capable of a purer love because mercenary love is a love born of fear.

Mercenary love is for the most part love of self, because it is directed at oneself, in search of what is useful to us personally: in other words, it is not "genuine" (c. 60). And, given the previous condition of slavery to the world and of continuous thought of carnal and earthly things, it always expects some material advantages to come from serving God, as a reward and result of its new condition (see c. 59). This is why we are invited to lift up our feet from the earth. The consolations or joys that God gives in this new state to support the weak might seem to encourage this imperfection of love. The soul, in fact, has lost fear of the "punishment that happens after the misdeed" (c. 59), the soul tastes the joy of forgiveness, spiritual peace. It experiences an unexpected pleasure in finding itself with God and with his friends (see c. 60) and in confiding in him. It enjoys other "delights" of the emotive and sensitive dimension, such as the aesthetic enjoyment of religious rites, a tangible fervor felt in devotions, etc. It appreciates the gratitude of those whom it has helped.

The signs of mercenary love are certain reactions which are easily verified (see c. 60). First, the scandal of impatience at the arrival of sensible sufferings and tribulations; some souls then relax their will to serve God because of no reward: "every little wind makes them sail away" (c. 59), taking them far away from what is good. The second sign is weariness in the battle against temptations (which still keep on afflicting them for a long time) because, in expecting easy gains, they flee from the strain "for fear of having to bear suffering" (c. 60). Third, the attenuation of fervor in prayer, as if prayer were no longer good because of the disappearance of consolations experienced before, "thinking to be deprived of God when in fact it feels deprived only in its mind of consolations and feelings" (letter 62). Therefore, it advances on the bridge "little by little" (c. 59; letter 272), that is, reluctantly, sluggishly, "with much tepidity" (c. 49; letter 272). Fourth, the diminution or cessation of works of mercy toward the neighbor, feeling it is not worthwhile because there is no just recognition or reciprocation. He who loves God with mercenary love, loves his neighbor in the same way (see c. 60).

Thus it happens that some, not wanting to comprehend their imperfection, turn back and fall into the river, as if they were pushed by two winds: the wind of prosperity which again draws them toward the disordered anxiety of making money only for the sake of making money, of success at any cost; and the wind of adversity that makes them discouraged and turn back "because of impatience, but not because the soul has hatred for its misdeed in offending me, but for fear of its own suffering" (c. 49; see c. 54).

From the Mercenary to the Faithful Servant

Things must not continue in this way: the soul must render account of everything if it is not to be lost. God indeed does not want it to relapse, on the contrary, that it rise to a love less imperfect. Here the Eternal Truth warns the soul: "All this happens to it because the root of self-love is not ripped out, and so they do not persevere" (c. 49). Here is sensitive self-love that does not see beyond the satisfactions and material gains which, quite naturally, impede the soul's surmounting of this egotistical and coarse obstacle. The crisis is entrusted to knowledge of self and of God—"If they do not recognize their imperfection..." (c. 60)—that has the job of discovering the trap of carnal self-love and revealing where God's desire is directed: "those who rise up [the bridge], with the feet of affection, stripped of servile fear. By doing so they become faithful servants..." (c. 59).

The soul must understand that, after coming out of the deadly water, if it does not replace fear of punishment with love of virtue, its love is defective and "since the soul cannot live without love, it returns to its miserable self-love" (letter 272). Stopping and sitting "at the entrance of the bridge" and "not adding a spark of fire to the knowledge of themselves and of the goodness of God in them," they fall into the most dangerous and grave lukewarmness (ibid.). Then, it is no wonder that, having forgotten the fear of punishment that made it vomit "the rottenness of sin" in confession, the sinner like the dog that returns to its vomit, lets himself be drawn by the desire of the corrupted things that he has thrown up (see c. 49).[107]

Since the most grievous and profound danger comes from sensuality or the perverse sensitive will, which ought to be a servant of reason (see c. 51) and instead is often rebelling against it and God, it is necessary to fight self-will, indeed kill it, otherwise it will kill us. This is done by being vigilant with the conscience, ready to reproach every disordered impulse; by taking the double-edged sword of hatred of vice and love of virtue; by never satisfying the pretentious claims of the senses, except when it is necessary for life, but rather counteracting them and trampling them in the affections; never giving the selfish will what it wants, albeit doing it with discretion but without weakness and self-pity (see letter 265).

In this crisis of aridity of the senses or lukewarmness God does not stay inactive, indeed he increases the crisis, seeking to wean the soul from its hyper-sensitivity, withdrawing the milk of the first consolations. He does this by training the soul in a life of pure and disinterested virtue and by leading it to a more perfect knowledge, first, of its own nothingness which claims nothing for itself and, then, of God's goodness which allows everything to happen for its good (see c. 60). Therefore, it is God's intention that this should be a crisis of growth provoked by a need for clarification and the desire to overcome the coarse imperfection of our own sentiments.[108] Therefore, when these aridities and tribulations come, let us look higher to the truth that God's love prods us forward because he no longer wants to treat us as salaried strangers but as faithful servants and then as his friends and sons (c. 60).[109]

The soul reaches the state of faithful servants, which is almost in between the first and second stair, when it passed the test of no longer serving the Lord by observing the commandments for fear of punishment but out of respect for the supreme goodness of the Creator. It no longer does good works solely for its own profit but now does so with less respect or regard for oneself. It also now tries to flee from sin not only because it offends God but also to acquire virtue which pleases God.

Once we reach the state of being faithful servants, the servile state proper to the first stair is over. Many things have been understood and appreciated in practice, in particular that of never trusting in self-love which is essentially contrary to the love of God (see letter 7) and that soon again self-love will be alive under other forms which will take us away from happiness. Therefore, "in whatever state that man finds himself, he needs to kill self-love" (c. 56).

CHAPTER SIX

THE CHRIST-BRIDGE: *SECOND STAIR*

The second stair is the *liberal* spiritual stage or state in respect to the first stage that was servile; it is *more perfect* in comparison to the first which was imperfect; it is characterized by the *love of a friend*; it is placed on Christ crucified at the wounded side and therefore is the stair of the *open side* (see letter 75).[110] The positive tendency that transformed the mercenary into the faithful servant is now more accentuated in the pursuit of virtue, above all the greatest virtue which is charity. This stage corresponds substantially with the illuminative way or of the proficient, but with its own character.[111]

The passage to the second stair is quite laborious and is not accomplished until the servant is changed into the friend and reaches the wounded side where the wayfarer discovers the secret of the heart. The ascent on the profile of Christ crucified is actuated because of an increased illumination. Jesus and his doctrine, seen at first only in the perspective of an escape from the evils of life, now appear more and more in a positive light of elevation, warmheartedness and an intimate bond of affection.

Love of the Virtues

"On the first stair, lifting the feet of affection from the earth, strip oneself of vice; on the second, clothe oneself with the love of virtue" (c. 26)

Being Clothed or Filled with Love

This is the sweet effort that the faithful servant is invited to make. To comprehend it and want it is a sign that one is invited and that the Lord wants to manifest himself (see cc. 60, 62), as the Lord himself says: "Whoever will love me will be one thing with me and I with him, and I will manifest myself and we will dwell together" (c. 60).[112]

It is now time to consider the virtues and the virtuous life in their positive value, i.e., not as an antidote of moral evils but as an enrichment of intrinsic goodness. Then we will understand that if souls "do not rise higher with love of the virtues, servile fear is unable to give them eternal life" (c. 58). The virtues, we recall, are the material of the bridge (see c. 27). Let us come to a better understanding of this detail of the allegory. The "true and real virtues" are living values made so by the power of the blood of Christ (that is to say, by his merits and grace), embedded as stones on the body of the incarnate Word, i.e., developed and solidified on the supporting framework of his doctrine. For this reason the bridge is called the "way of truth" (cc. 29, 42, 50, 54, etc.), in the sense that salvation is not to be found in purely external assistance but in "intrinsic" virtues (see c. 9) matured in our soul by the convergence of grace and our conscious imitation of Christ.

To comprehend the value of the virtues is to dispose oneself to love them and desire to make them increase in oneself, since for the human person it is natural to desire the true good unless we let ourselves be blinded and deceived by self-love (see c. 44). The virtues are the human person's true wealth, a richness to be acquired and increased (see letter 345). True virtue is loved and found, first of all, "in the knowledge of the goodness of God" and with the kind of search and practice that must be above all interior: "In him we will acquire virtue, seeking it within our soul; elsewhere and in no other way will we ever find it" (letter 345). Virtues increase if "the fire of holy desire" for them increase in us, the fire being fed by always throwing on it the "firewood" of the memory of the gifts received from God, "and most especially the gift of the blood of the Word, his only begotten Son" (letter 290). We need always to join together "true love of virtue and hated of vice" (c. 65); furthermore, we must not forget prayer through which "the soul acquires every virtue with true perseverance" (c. 66).

Love for God

"It is not enough to flee from sin out of fear of punishment, nor to embrace virtues because of their usefulness, as it is not sufficient to give us eternal life; but you must give up sin, because sin displeases me, and love virtue for my sake" (c. 60). Virtue for the sake of self-interest and virtue for the sake of virtue are both imperfect and incapable of bringing forth perseverance. Valid only are the "virtues founded on love" (c. 49) and as such the faithful servant must seek them.

The faithful servant enjoys increasingly the pleasure of serving God and, knowing his goodness better now, he or she receives everything looking less at the gift and the hands which offer it and more to the giver (see letters 62, 146; c. 72). If we persist in this way of looking, our service changes into love and thus the servant becomes the friend (see c. 60).[113] To facilitate the soul's recognition of the affection of the giver in the gift, the Lord wanted to "unite the gift and the Giver," by making himself man, so that now we cannot have one without seeing the other (see c. 72). So it is that Christ is the bridge of virtue by means of the attraction of love.

The Risks of Imperfect Love

Love of the virtues has its merits and its dangers, and the foremost danger is to linger in its advantages. This does not mean that the merits are not truly such but only that they must be understood as transit points to reach something higher and securer, i.e., to go now from the feet to the side of Christ.

The Consolations of God[114]

We have already noted the joys of the first good way of living; now, as we advance toward the second stair with love of the virtues, there are some others. First, when the soul's interior faculties are gathered together in the good works which correspond to each of the three, the Gospel promise (Mt 18:20) is actuated: "Then by grace I rest among them" (c. 51; see c. 54).[115] This is felt in the soul: "Then Jesus appears to the soul through feeling, letting us touch him with humble and continual prayer" (letter 173).[116] At this point God adds different ways in which he makes himself felt and enjoyed through our feelings by means of the affection of charity and the sweetness of prayer (see c. 61). Catherine mentions a notable variety of ways (see c. 68). Overall, it can be said that these many consoling effects are all apart from grace[117] but come to us instead "through sentiment (=feeling)," such as: the thirst for virtue and for the honor of God and the salvation of souls (see c. 54); the hunger or desire for sacramental food (see c. 61); the tears of sweetness of one who is moved by the charity of God and of neighbor (see c. 89), although this may be sensitive spiritual weeping (see cc. 90, 95).

Attachment to Consolations

Since consolations have a spiritual origin, it is very easy for the soul to be naively attached to them; in this case consolations become "thorns that prick the soul which loves and possesses [these joys] in a disordered way" (c. 58). The deceit comes from self-love that shows itself to still be alive, taking the form of attachment to spiritual things because of the delight coming from them.[118] Thus the soul exchanges the Lord for that which is only a gift freely given by him and now seeks above all the gift, thinking: "I would like to have this in order to possess God more fully" (letter 17). This new danger of blindness to self-love constitutes an interference between our heart and God's perfect love which must be "without anything in between" (letter 94, etc.), except the neighbor. It is, therefore, also an impediment to charity toward one's neighbor whenever we do not sacrifice our own habits or spiritual comforts to help others who are in need, not understanding that God is found rather in the love of neighbor than in love of spiritual consolations (see c. 69) and that it is better to be without consolations than without love.

Many souls stop at this point and do not make any more progress, remaining in the mediocrity of a love that is still servile, and often returning to a lower stage because they do not understand the gravity of the obstacle to be overcome. Here also God intervenes, provoking the inevitable crisis with the temporary withdrawal of consolations so as to bring souls to a better comprehension. This is the trial of the "sterile mind" or of spiritual aridity, of which we must now speak of at length because it is a normal but also painful and useful phenomenon at this point of the spiritual journey.[119]

The Battles of the Sterile Mind (Aridity)[120]

We have already seen on the first stair some purifying trials similar to aridity; however, the experience of aridity is really proper to the second stair, directed as it is to the purification of the interior sentiments and to prepare for attaining to the love of the friend. Let us set aside temptations, which we have already spoken about, that imperfect souls often cause themselves by their imprudence. Here we will examine especially the trials which are independent of personal responsibility. The characteristics of these trials are: they come and go suddenly without any recognizable cause on the part of the individual (see c. 144); the sense of apparent abandonment on the part of God (ibid.), of spiritual emptiness, of the mind's darkness (see letters 26, 213, 221, etc.); the mind is incapacitated and seems dry and sterile (see letters 65, 71; c. 144) not having a single good thought able to awaken the feelings.

Description of the Phenomenon

Everything happens in the sphere of sentiment, Catherine says, particularly in the experiential field of the internal senses; and it occurs in two directions: the disappearance of the feeling of God's presence and the arrival of disturbing thoughts.

It seems to the soul as if it had been totally abandoned by me, without any feeling; the soul seems to be neither in the world [of sin], because it is actually not there, nor in me because it has no feeling at all except the feeling that its will does not want to offend God [with any sin].   (c. 144)

Everything seems tasteless and senseless; no internal faculty seems capable of turning to God for anything (ibid.), as if he were so far off that the soul cannot succeed in putting itself before him (see letter 65). The situation is painful, not only because the soul no longer feels delight in its devotions and in other spiritual things but has, in fact, the impression that every one of its actions is dishonest and corrupt, so much so that the soul is close to hell (see c. 144), without faith and charity. The desolation is complete for the fact that God does not answer any prayer and leaves the soul in darkness of the mind, finding no particular fault in itself and feeling rejected by God (ibid.).

Yet God permits the sterile mind to be tormented "with many troubling and different thoughts" (c. 144; see letter 221) coming from one's self-will or self-love and from the devil. The "will causes the storm [=unrest]" (letter 17) and is often recalcitrant, not actually refusing to be troubled but preferring to be troubled in its own way, when and where it wants, because otherwise it thinks it will lose God or offend him by doing what it does not enjoy (letter 71). Moreover, spiritual consolations seem to the imperfect soul a sign of devotion and its indispensable source of nourishment and not having them is to be "in pain, in bitterness and in affliction and in the greatest tedium" (ibid.). Also, in practicing the external virtues such as works of charity or corporal penances, souls unconsciously feed their spiritual self-will, believing themselves to be full of God when they are feeling joy in doing things their own way; if, however, they are deprived of the possibility of doing them or if they no longer feel any sweetness, they become desperate just as if they were damned (see letter 213). Or, in the great variety of delights that God dispenses, the will demands the repetition of those it has already enjoyed, "as if it wanted to impose laws on the Holy Spirit" (c. 68); otherwise it seems to be in hell, feeling tempted and deprived of extraordinary graces that God had granted it at another time (see c. 70).[121]

Besides the usual temptations, God permits the devil to insinuate all kinds of disturbing thoughts of desperation and unconditional surrender by telling the soul: This life is not made for you, it is too hard and difficult for you; it requires another temperament; If the Lord had given you health and time, things would be different. Or, the devil proposes that we give up the weapon of prayer, confusing our thoughts with what appears to be common-sense reasoning such as: What is the use now of praying like this? It is better to do it when you're well disposed (see letters 71, 169; c. 65); or worse, the suggestion that we give up prayer entirely, saying: Who ever listens to you? You are so bad and your prayers cannot possibly please God (see letters 71, 221, 3335).

The devil also tempts the imperfect soul with the illusion, under the pretence of loving quiet and spiritual recollection when in fact it is trying to escape from suffering, that one could go to the Father without going through the suffering of the incarnate Son, whose way is the cross (see c. 53; letters 318, 335, etc.). Sometimes he also causes blasphemous images or similar things to flash in the mind even though the soul does not consent although it fears having done so, "otherwise it has no pain except for the fear of having offended God" (letter 335). The devil's work can be summed up as *mental confusion* inasmuch as it makes the soul incapable of judgment, serenity, or living a peaceful life for fear of sinning or having sinned or because of the weariness of aridity. It is important to know that "mental confusion is worse than all the other defects" (letter 178; see c. 144) because it dries up the soul and removes all goodwill (see letter 335).

The Reasons

The actual reasons for this trial all pertain to greater enlightenment and understanding and better discipline of the will. The trial is meant to lead us to a humbler and perfect knowledge of our own fragility and unworthiness and of the infinite goodness of God who permits everything for our good (see cc. 60, 64, 70): "We know both of these [=ourselves and God] better during times of struggle and aridity" (letter 71), seeing that we are incapable of freeing ourselves from these struggles and that God strengthens our will so that we do not give up (see letters 221, 26).

Another reason God allows trials is to destroy, with the help of the above-mentioned knowledge, "our sensitive self-will, cloaked under a spiritual mantle" (letter 71), which shows itself to be alive by its desire for consolations (see c. 63), so that the soul might now rise to a more disinterested and perfect love (see cc. 68-70), considering itself undeserving of spiritual peace and of being listened to or having its wishes satisfied.

God does not free the soul from suffering as soon as he is called upon so as to prevent the soul from attributing it to itself. God allows the soul to be tried and purified "in the light of faith" so that we will believe that providence permits everything for our good and put our trust only in God because no other can help us in these struggles (see cc. 63,144). Everything becomes gradually clearer, as Eternal Truth says: "And then I return to you with more light and knowledge of my truth" (c. 64).

The Behavior of the Soul

The soul must be guided by the conviction that mental confusion must never prevail over faith and knowledge. In fact, the trial is solely inspired by God's love for us; he neither permits or wants the grace in our souls to be in danger nor the demons to clamor outside the fortress of the will (see c. 144). The battle is a test of faith and love on our part in which we show our pure and undiluted attachment to the Lord (ibid.). The trials do not last long: just as they come unexpectedly they cease suddenly so that we may realize that they come from God and therefore "come and go" in accordance with what God judges as useful to the soul (see c. 144; letter 71), even returning many times: "every now and then I withdraw from the soul, not by grace but by feeling" (c. 63).

There are some good rules suggested by faith and prudence. First, we must stand firm in the humble knowledge of oneself, feeling unworthy of consider-ation or reward, "thinking oneself to deserve punishments and struggles and unworthy of the fruit that follows the pain. Out of humility the soul regards itself unworthy of mental peace and quiet" (letter 33).

Second, we must persevere in fidelity to one's own duties and to good works, especially for the good of one's neighbor even when painful and apparently pointless (see c. 144), knowing that in persevering "the soul profits more in times of bitterness and suffering...than in times of sweetness" (letter 71; see letter 62).

Third, we must, above all, persevere in prayer even when it is not enjoyable because it "is the weapon with which we defend ourselves, or let us say a bond that ties and fortifies our will in God and increases fortitude with the most ardent charity" (letter 169; see letters 71, 335, 353). The proof that prayer alone does this by itself, apart from any feeling, is in the fact that if this weapon is put down, "the devil can gradually get from us what he wants" (letter 169). Moreover, we must recognize that "if the soul mostly gives up this [exercise of prayer] or some virtuous act, it is a sign that its love is mercenary, namely that it loves only for its own consolation and that love of one's own spiritual delight is still rooted in its soul" (letter 263).

Fourth, we must await "with living faith" the return of normality (c. 63), that ends "the time of darkness, since from darkness is born the light" (letter 211), just as "by the opposite of virtue one acquires virtue" (ibid.).[122]

The Love of the Friend and the Secret of the Heart

The one who overcomes the trial of aridity or is prepared to fight effectively the battles of the sterile mind is already on the second stair because by now he is animated by a love that is not servile, the love of the friend, and has arrived at the wound on the side of Christ where the secret of the heart is discovered.

The Love of the Friend

Charity is friendship love or the mutual affection that exists between God and the human person, according to St. Thomas Aquinas.[123] Catherine recognizes friendship love at this point on the journey, when one has arrived at an authentic love, or as she calls it, "sincere and liberal" (c. 65).

The love of the friend is more perfect than that of the preceding servile love because it is love "without respect of oneself," that is, without regard to oneself (c. 56). It is a love of pure benevolence, as the Scholastics said. It is the love of a reciprocal fusion of the soul and reciprocal communion of thoughts and feelings: "secret things are made known to the friend, who is made one with his friend" (c. 60). The reciprocity of affection on the part of God is formally assured: "I respond to your love with the love by which I am loved" (c. 60).

The dynamic exigencies of charity, discovered in knowledge of oneself and of God, have brought the faithful servant to this state if he or she has looked beyond the gift to the affection of the Giver and has proved it in battle. Thus the faithful servant realized: "It is true that the servant can grow through his virtue and love which will bring him to the Lord, where he becomes the dearest friend" (c. 60). Catherine shows this dynamic with the irrepressible expression, which we have already heard, that sets fire to the stages of the spiritual journey: "I want to show you in what way he comes to be a friend: and being made a friend he is made a child, attaining filial love" (c. 63). But it is clear that he who has achieved the love of the friend "has climbed with the feet of affection and has reached the secret of the heart, that is, the second of the three stairs" (ibid.).

On the other hand, it is clear that Catherine places filial love at the third stair and mercenary love at the first (c. 56). In the journey's triple division she intends to say that the soul "from the servile state arrives at the liberal, and from the liberal state arrives at the filial" (ibid.). Elsewhere she distinguishes only the "true servant, true friend and true son" (letter 94); and later specifies that, after servile and mercenary love, one arrives at the love of the friend (see c. 60) and this can only be on the second stair: "he who arrives at the love of the friend...has climbed the feet of affection and has arrived at the secret of the heart, that is, at the second of the three stairs" (c. 63). Therefore, only if one considers the faithful servant as an intermediate state between the mercenary and the friend can we speak of this as the third stage (see c. 78), but only the friend occupies the second stair and nowhere else but the second.

Let us see what the friend does (see c. 63).

First, the friend loves virtue and every good thing only for love of God (see c. 60).

Second, the friend enjoys: the manifestations of God in his soul, namely (see c. 60) the manifestation of the Son in the incarnation and in the redeeming blood, felt in the soul as a personal effusion; the manifestation of multiple charisms (such as the spirit of prophecy) made through the channel of charity ("through the affection of love) or other spiritual delights already mentioned (spiritual joy, living contrition, intellectual illuminations, etc.; see c. 78); the manifestations of the invisible missions of the divine Persons when the soul seeks and finds them in prayer and according to the measure of holy desire.

Third, when God withdraws, the soul "is locked in the house of knowledge of oneself. And there, with living faith awaits the descent of the Holy Spirit" like the disciples in the Upper Room (c. 66; see c. 73),[124] keeping watch so as to correct and regulate thoughts and actions according to charity and, above all, praying "continually with the prayer of a good and holy will; this is continuous prayer" (c. 63).

Fourth, the friend's love pours forth on the neighbor, with ardor and perfection proportioned to his or her friendship with God, i.e., without fear or servile love because to whatever extent we love God perfectly we also love our neighbor (see c. 64). Catherine notes that the pure love of neighbor is like one who fills a pot in the running water of a fountain and drinks without removing it from the flow of water so that it is never emptied, meaning that the soul must never be detached from the love of God otherwise the love of neighbor will dry up. The soul also never detaches itself from love of neighbor just because it has nothing to gain or because of little return.

Fifth, he enjoys the sweetness of the tears of the perfect (see cc. 88-89) which is a perfect form of weeping because it comes from warmhearted love.

The Secret of the Heart

The secret of the heart is the true finishing line of friendship love and it is placed where the second stair stops, that is, where it fully arrives: at the wounded side. "He who arrives at the love of the friend...has arrived at the secret of the heart, that is, at the second of the three stairs" (c. 63). Why secret? Because the soul is enclosed in the cavern of Christ's side and because it is reserved for the friend, given that "secret things are made known to friends" (c. 60), alluding to the word of Christ: "I do not call you servants any longer...but I have called you friends, because I have made known to you everything that I have heard from my Father" (Jn 15:15).

The secret of the heart placed at the wounded side is a spiritual image frequently found in medieval piety and religious writings. However, as Catherine frequently uses the expression it refers, above all, to St. Bernard of Clairvaux's commentary on the *Song of Songs*: "Patet arcanum cordis per foramina corporis" ["The inner sanctum of the heart is revealed through the clefts of the body"].[125] With respect to the religion of the heart as a symbol of love, it foreshadows the modern devotion of the Sacred Heart without, however, proposing Christ's wound or heart as an object of veneration.

The wounded side of Christ is a *channel* and a *window* (see letter 127) and a *cavern*. It is a channel through which we receive the blood of grace, drawn entirely from his sacred humanity: "heart and soul and body of Jesus Christ." It is a window to which we must fix our gaze so as to see the goodness of God in us; that is, the visual medium through which the secret inside is made known and recognized (see c. 54; letter 318). It is a cavern, that is to say a mystical refuge of the soul to shelter itself from its enemies, where one hides in oneself, resting and enjoying the quietness of the soul (see letters 47, 308).

76

In the great wound the friend makes the discovery of the heart and recognizes love's proper place, i.e., the soul is made conscious of an aspect with a double objective: the warmhearted love of God for us, and the authenticity of our love directed to God. The secret of the heart is first of all a mystical revelation of divine love: "He finds the warmhearted love of true and real virtues in the open heart; through which opening is made known to us the warmhearted and fiery love, making for us a bath of his blood" (letter 309). This is for several reasons. First, because the wound on Christ's side seems to be the most appropriate way to show the open heart and wound of love (see c. 26), as the Lord himself explained to Catherine: "I wanted you to see the secret of the heart, showing it open to you, so that you could see what I could not show you through finite suffering: that I loved you even more [than that]" (c. 75). Second, because the truth of the Father's love, as we have seen, is manifested in the blood, given abundantly up to the point of being pierced by the lance (see letters 308, 309, etc.), a love that was shown to be infinite, especially in the wound received after death as well as the blood that poured forth (see c. 75; letters 8, 11, 12, 16, 34, etc.). Third, it is a mystical revelation of God's love because it makes known that it is a matter of warmhearted love, i.e., not conventional but felt, warm, inflamed (see letters 74, 309, 318; c. 54, etc.). Fourth, because the opening of the heart signifies an opening of intimate affection and of confidence (see c. 60), it was as if one offered oneself to be searched from within and to take a look into the heart of the Giver of every heavenly gift (see letter 146).

The secret of the heart is also, by reflection, a revelation of our heart (perhaps in accordance with the inter-communicability of the double knowledge of self and of God), i.e., of our capacity to respond to the solicitation of God's love. In fact, "having climbed onto the feet of affection, the soul begins to taste the affection of the heart, putting the eye of the intellect on the open heart of my Son, where consummated and ineffable love is found" (c. 26). The faithful servant is by now conscious of having in his or her heart friendship love, so different from that of servile love; and when one will be purified of every form of mercenary self-love, God himself will recognize that person as a real friend:

> [B]y doing so they will please me so very much that through this they will arrive at friendship love. And so I will make myself known to them.... This is the condition of the dearest friend: there are now two bodies and one soul through the affection of love; because love transforms one into what one loves.(c. 60)

And here is how the soul is illumined by the light that comes from the friend: "If he is made one soul [with only the friend], nothing of [him] can be secret" (ibid.). This is an assurance of heavenly communications that come

77

from seeing and feeling everything with the key of love, above all during prayer which becomes more and more a search for intimacy with God (see c. 61) and a need to penetrate and love the secrets of the friend.

This revelation of one's own charity—that is, the discovery that our heart, which seemed so alienated from the Lord and unable to love him even minimally, having now encountered his heart—is renewed experientially ("This I have now found again…in the feeling of my soul," letter 146) every time that one meditates deeply on the fact that God is love, or when one looks more at his affection than to hand that gave us his gifts, in other words in the loving knowledge of the "the consumed heart of the sweet and good Jesus," that leaves our heart "inflamed and clothed with fire" (ibid). Furthermore, in the side of Christ the soul becomes aware of its own dignity, i.e., of being, after baptism, "kneaded in the blood of the Lamb" and the object of an infinite love and desire (c. 75). To this love and desire must correspond a love that has something of the infinite, at least in the desire to unite with God "through the affection of love" (c. 3), since desire and affection are the only infinite things that the soul possesses (see c. 92).

Conclusion

This, then, is why the Seraphic Virgin, Catherine of Siena, exhorts us: "Put, put your mouth on the side of the Son of God, because it is a mouth that spews forth the fire of charity."[126] Indeed, "the soul that rests and gazes with the eye of intellect at the heart consumed and open because of love receives in itself so much conformity to him, seeing itself loved so much, that it can do no other but love" (letter 97). It is the invitation to hide oneself in the cavern of the side (see letters 47, 72, 308) or "in the burning heart, consumed and opened, like a window…which is never closed" (letter 97). This is the place where the friends of God must stay if they are to be truly themselves, and there "in that opened heart is found my charity and charity for your neighbor," not only in theory or in the memory but in "seeing and tasting this love" (c. 124).

CHAPTER SEVEN

THE CHRIST-BRIDGE: THIRD STAIR

"Many were seen beginning to climb up.... And many, responding to the first call, reached the second [stair], but few were seen to reach the greatest perfection" (c. 57). We have already seen the reason why the many are reduced to the few. Now let us see what these few have obtained and, therefore, what has been lost by many. We shall see all the reasons for desiring to be among those who put no limit or reserve on love. The bridge was cast between two shores with an integral finality expressed in the vertical plane by its three finishing lines, the first two being the reason for the last: "So the bridge has three stairs, so that by climbing the first and the second we can reach the last" (c. 26).

The third stair is generally characterized by: *filial love* which is perfect love, "I say that filial love is perfect, because in the love of the son [=the creature] one receives the inheritance from me, the Eternal Father" (c. 63); *peace and quiet* which ensue after the battles against the vices and self-love which occupied the journey before now; *most perfect union* that surpasses every affection and feeling. Then there are particular characteristics, some of which pertain to the preceding stair and which Catherine assigns to a *first state* on the third stair; other characteristics, more distinct and secure, form part of a *second state* on the third stair and more properly belong to that stair (see cc. 74, 78). These form two successive and contiguous states—the *perfect state* (=third state) and the *state of most perfect union* (=fourth state)—both of which are on this final stair, and one cannot exist without the other (ibid.).[127]

The fact is that in fluid and evolving situations, as is the case of this spiritual journey, it is difficult to make clear-cut distinctions of the different phases because the passages from one to the other are not made in increments, like a clock, but instead the last elements of the preceding phase are in the beginning of the following one. Therefore we cannot insist on absolute subdivisions, which in the Catherinian text do not have a clear and distinct content, but rather we must follow the profile of ever clearer characters proper to filial love and the filial state in which the highest stair consists.

To the Mouth By Way of the Heart

"Then one rises with the most ardent desire and arrives at another stair, that is to the mouth, and there one rests in peace and quiet, and enjoys peace" (letter 75).

Love demands no stopping on the journey; however, its passage to the highest stair is not sudden or simple. The wounded side has revealed the secret of an infinite love and desire that Jesus had and has for us, with such a communication of affections that the soul "knows and acquires so much fire of love that immediately it runs to the third" stair (c. 76). The word "immediately" is indicative of the Catherinian logic which is not about time but about the consequence of a thing. How does it happen? It is again knowledge that precedes love. The soul, in fact, has arrived at the side "leaving behind imperfect love for the knowledge that derives from warmhearted love" (ibid.). It is now that such love as discovered at the wounded side exercises its attraction. Which way does the soul go? Catherine says: "through the heart," which is to say the heart of Christ. And how does it go? "By remembrance of the blood where one is re-baptized" (ibid.) This is a truly significant transit which is like a re-baptism. The way to the ultimate perfection passes through the heart of Christ and is a moving forward in the footsteps of his love, marked out by his blood, "seeing, enjoying and experiencing the fire of my charity" (c. 76), says the Lord.

The saying "by remembrance of the blood where one is re-baptized" is worth noting because it helps us understand how the reference (see c. 75) to baptism serves to underscore the new extensions of the sacrament's value and reach, which go from conversion (coming out of the river) up to the soul's great perfection. It is a sign that the journey of perfection is a normal development of the first grace and of the universal call of the baptized to salvation.[128]

Purification of Love

We have learned by now that this progress is a sublimation or purification of love. But what does this transformation that brings the soul to the highest goal consist of? Let us be aware that there is "no one in this life, no matter how perfect, who cannot grow to a greater perfection" (c. 145). The perfect can become the most perfect. The law of progress requires that this growth is never arrested. First of all, divine providence takes the initiative and we will see how the soul must collaborate with it, that is to say by observing the *signs* of a good spiritual journey and by obeying the *promptings of grace* (ibid.). In the mean time, providence seeks to conserve and test perfect souls in their perfection and in "making them to grow continually" (ibid.) through the assiduous work of gradual improvement. Chief among the signs of a good spiritual journey are trials; and chief among the promptings of grace is the *hunger and thirst for souls.*[129]

Let us first consider the trials. "Sorrow grows in the person who grows in love" (cc. 5, 145), sorrow for all those who are in danger on their own spiritual journeys, sorrow for those we love, and sorrow that can occur in friendship. There are trials that serve to prune the branches so that they will give more fruit (see c. 145)[130] and are for the sake of an increase of love: *external trials* such as tribulations, injuries, loss of things that are more necessary to one's corporal and social life; *internal trials* such as temptations of the flesh and diabolical disturbances which, however, neither touch the depth of the soul nor affect the will. The external trials serve to foster the growth of patience, preventing it from growing rusty; a patience that is not only endurance but a living expression of grief for the offence made to God by the soul's affronts as well as for the damage done to the sinner. The interior trials of the passions foster the growth of the faithful soul in knowledge, humility, and in understanding those who are troubled like itself (ibid.).[131]

Second, the hunger and thirst for souls is both a prompting of grace and a torment suited to purify the soul. Owing to Divine Love, this hunger and thirst increases in the soul and it has an ever greater concern for its neighbor, thereby demonstrating the soul's love of God according to the principle already mentioned: "every good work and every action was done by means [=through] of your neighbor " (c. 145).[132] The emphasis placed on the "means," i.e., the neighbor, comes closer to the divine ideal "to love gratuitously and not out of debt" (c. 64) in which one seeks to do good to others without regard to oneself and "without expecting any benefit" (ibid.).[133]

Love now goes further: no longer having any regard for oneself to the point of not minding the suffering that one encounters for sake of one's neighbors (see c. 76) and to love them in such a way as not to feel the weight of the effort or the suffering involved because every other evil seems minor compared to that of the loss of a soul (see c. 145); and even "if it were possible to escape hell, have paradise, and leave this world without any suffering they would not want to" because they desire earnestly to follow the crucified Christ (letter 335). This divine passion for souls imitates that of the apostles who, after Pentecost, completely lost every fear and announced the truth of Christ with courage and were happy to suffer for it (see c. 74). So the true servants and friends of God love to eat the food of souls, i.e., to seek after their salvation on the table of the cross (see letter 64; cc. 76, 124, etc.).

Intermediate Phases

Before arriving to enjoy the peace of the mouth of Christ, arriving at the maximum stability in charity and every other virtue, the following takes place:

First, little by little the "game of love" of the soul's feeling of God that comes and goes ceases; the fluctuations of this kind tend to disappear through the arrival of a presence of love stronger and firmer.

Second, "the sensitive will remains dead" (c. 76) and that is why every movement of corrupted nature, in the senses and in the spirit, has been resolutely corrected and despoiled of every imperfection (see c. 73). The purgative work is terminated since the transition can be accomplished only when the soul's "self-will has died" (c. 76), not before. This means that the death of self-will is a secure index of the moment in which the feet are put on the third stair and one passes into the number of the most perfect: "the sign that they have arrived is this: that self-will died when they tasted the affection of my charity" (ibid.); the war to destroy the last roots of self-love which lasted throughout the stop or settling-down on the second stair has ceased: "Having climbed to the second [stair] the soul arrives at the third, that is, at the mouth, where it finds peace after the previous great war that had been caused by its own faults" (c. 26); the death of every type of egoism occurs, meaning the definitive defeat and subjection of sensuality and self-love so that the mind is no longer in their grip and disturbed by them; for example, the sufferings and labors of doing good works are no longer painful because the will has died (see c. 76); in fact, the soul "is deprived of pain because it has removed from itself that which causes pain, that is to say self-will founded on self-love" (letter 108); the result is a kind of indifference to things that once troubled or lured us, and so souls are at peace because by now they are as unmoved by consolation as by sufferings (see c. 77; letter 263).

Third, it is as if one's self-will is transferred to God, always conforming itself more perfectly to his will. Nothing is actually destroyed but purified: "This is because the ordered will is alive in me, clothed with my eternal will, the sensitive will having died" (c. 76). The Lord praises this conformity which continues to concretize the perfect union of the son with the Father: the son experiences prosperous and adverse things in the same way "because he finds my will in everything and he thinks of doing nothing else, no matter where he is, but to conform himself to it" (c. 77). It is in this sense that one speaks of losing oneself in God. This love of conformity to the will of God gradually consolidates beginning from the first steps on the bridge, little by little, until creatures see with the "pupil of faith" that God wants their sanctification and "in seeing they know and in knowing they love and in loving they annihilate and lose their self-will. Having lost it, they clothe themselves with my will" (c. 45).[134]

From the Friend to the Son

Distinctive Characters

The distinctive characters of these two types and grades of love, i.e. the third and fourth states, are not altogether clear. One reason is that in the filial state the substance of the friend persists. However, there are differences, as Catherine herself indicates, and they are partly perceptible in the process she describes. The soul's union with God, as we will see in a moment, is certainly the essential element of filial charity; it results negatively from the suppression of self-love and positively from conformity to God's will. The figure of the son will result from details which emerge from comparison with the friend, although Catherine warns us that both friend and son "are united together, that the one is not without the other, just as my charity is not without charity for one's neighbor, and charity of neighbor is not without my charity" (c. 74; see c. 78). According to Catherine, we could say that the son is a friend with an additional importance: filial love is like a fruit of friendship love, the latter condition being partly still imperfect (see c. 78).

We could ask why, having placed the third stage of love at the mouth, Catherine did not prefer the term of "spouse" rather to that of son. In the first place, if the origin of the allegory was a text of St. Bernard which speaks of the kiss at the feet, the hand, and the mouth, such an orientation would be justified.[135] But spousal love, although it is perhaps the most expressive type of love owing to its intensity, does not work in this case because, being the maximum expression of carnal and sensual love, it could not represent effectively without confusion the most spiritual and perfect love that can be conceived.

The Differences Between the Friend and the Son

To understand the differences, let us first see in what sense the son is more perfect than the friend with regard to his condition and charity.

First, we note the differences in the *condition or state of life and spiritual perfection* (see letter 94) of the son compared to the friend:

The first way regards the right of inheritance, as Catherine expressly says: "I say that filial love is perfect because in the love of the son one receives the inheritance of myself, the Eternal Father" (c. 63). It means that the state of the son has the certainty of possession and already a share in the use of that which is the wealth of the Father; while the friend has nothing but the communication of sentiments and affections (c. 60).[136] The state of the son is firm and stable, linked to a bond that is above the fleeting tenderness of friendship and the fluctuations of sentiment: "To such as these has been removed the feeling of separation from me" (c. 78); "I will never withdraw from them through sentiment, rather their minds will always feel me in them, whereas with the others, as I told you, I go and return but only through sentiment and not by grace" (ibid.). In the son is realized the "great perfection" (c. 78) and the perfect union that is not found in the friend: there is in fact the "congregation [=gathering together]" of the soul's three powers, all filled with God (see c. 79) and one continually tastes the presence of the three divine Persons working in the soul (see c. 78). The son and the "most perfect" souls, described in Catherine's teaching of the three states, are synonymous and indicate the maximum perfection on earth, in which the soul already has the pledge of eternal life like an anticipation of the son's own inheritance, that although "being mortal tastes the reward of the immortals" (c. 79).

The second difference between the *charity* of the son and the friend is that filial love is perfect love, as already mentioned. Let us look at some of the reasons for this. Filial love is perfect because it is not only the sentiment and tenderness of love (as a matter of fact, the son reaches a point that he scorns spiritual consolations and charisms; see c. 78; letter 94), being that self-will is by this time dead, but it is love of perfect conformity to the will of the Father.

Filial love is perfect because it is a love that seems to identify itself with fire: "like a piece of burning coal that is completely consumed in the furnace, so that no one can take it or blow it out, because he is completely turned into fire" (c. 78). So it seems that at this point the soul becomes immune to earthly dangers because nothing of itself is exposed to the assaults of its enemies: "So these souls are thrown into the furnace of my charity, with nothing remaining outside of me, no one can take them away or drag them out of my grace because they have been made one with me and I with them" (c. 78).

Filial love is perfect because it is charity extended to all creatures, just like the charity of the Eternal Father. This charity is a requirement of sincere charity found at every stage but which here becomes, above all, impelling: "The soul enamored with my truth never tires of being useful to the entire world, both in general and in particular" (c. 7). In the pierced open heart the soul found the charity of God and that of the neighbor (c. 124), in which the latter is understood to be like the response of love to love. The love of those who are sons is now conformed or almost mystically identified with the Father and the Son, and they regard their neighbor in a new way. They "search for a way to be conformed to Christ crucified, and of nourishing oneself with his shame and toil and suffering," and together they "follow the Father's footprints, finding delight in charity to the neighbor," that is to say loving everyone, good and bad, "because they are rational creatures created by God and redeemed by one and the same blood as theirs" (letter 94), and they love without expecting to be loved by them (see c. 89).

The strong apostolic tendency of this entire "way of truth," i.e., the bridge, comes from the consideration of the neighbor at every spiritual level as a "means" in which we put into practice and make known our love of God, therefore like the back-and-forth response of a monastic choir in which the soul's progress in loving God is revealed according to the often repeated principle: every virtue and every vice is done by means of the neighbor (see c. 64).[137] If, therefore, every perfection is attained by means of the neighbor, the soul that, at the gates of heaven, participates perfectly in the desire of the Father and of Christ to give to souls eternal life is driven by a fearless charity "to give birth to the virtues for the neighbor" (c. 74), in other words to make the virtues which have been conceived interiorly to leave the house of the soul and to pour forth in external actions that benefit our neighbor. In this way we see that there is no height of perfection that would ever isolate anyone from others. Indeed, such perfect souls "can be called another Christ crucified" in a charismatic sense "because they have undertaken his office," which means to reconcile people among themselves and with God by praying, speaking, suffering and giving their good example (c. 146).

Perfect Union (=Third State) and the Sweet Signs[138]

Concerning this state of union—which is situated on the stair to Christ's mouth in part for logistical reasons and for symbolic reasons (which she analyzes in c. 76, so as to remain on line with her allegorical schema)—Catherine gives several annotations, stopping for a moment to consider the signs or the virtues proper to the state, some mystical phenomena, and the tears of the most perfect and the tears of fire.

The Perfect Union

Let us see how one reaches this third state, the first of two on the third stair, and then what it is like. First, the fact of the transformation of the disciples at Pentecost suggests some analogies, in a Catherinian key (see cc. 66, 73), without insinuating that this transition may be a pure mystical grace. "As Peter and the others were shut up in the house, just so those who have attained to the love of the Father, those who are sons, have done and must do the same thing" (letter 94).[139] The process is typically Catherinian and moral, but does not refer to a brief period like a spiritual retreat as the Pentecostal analogy would suggest if understood in an overly material way. The process is about the fullness of charity for God and neighbor, attained after an exercise of holy desire, always more intense, for Holy Communion, whether sacramental or virtual (see c. 66).[140] "The disciples and Peter lost their imperfection by keeping vigil, praying, and acquiring perfection" (ibid) that was sealed by the descent of the Holy Spirit. In the same way the soul must close itself up in the double cell of knowledge (see letter 94; cc. 66, 73) and await the Spirit's coming, being vigilant in the practice of the virtues and in continuous prayer, i.e., in directing all its actions to the glory of God (see letter 94).[141]

The union, which arrives like the Spirit of Pentecost, is the greatest and the most perfect union in this life, although it is imperfect in comparison to that of heaven (see c. 96); it is also susceptible of growth on this plane (see c. 146). Let us examine the characteristics of the perfect union, the third state.

First, perfect union is a *union of the mind* with God. The soul is completely immersed in God ("nothing remaining outside of me," c. 78), so much that God is like its atmosphere, its entire world of thoughts and interests: "the eternal deity...is to them a peaceful sea where the soul is so much in union [with God] that the mind has no movement other than in me" (c. 79). By "mind" is understood all the faculties of the soul together, elevated up to God and filled with him: "Then the memory is filled with nothing else but me; the intellect is elevated and gazes into the object of my truth; affection, which follows the intellect, loves and unites itself to that which the eye of the intellect sees" (c. 79).

Second, perfect union is also a *union of sentiment* or feeling with God since the Lord says: "I repose continually through grace and through sentiment in their soul" (c. 78): such souls always feel that God is in them and are never deprived of this sentiment (see cc. 78, 79). This is an interior perception of presence that is entirely spiritual and never ceases. The "sentiment of the body" is a different thing (c. 79; letter 263), which is a fact of the external senses which one can lose momentarily as, for example, in ecstasy (see letter 263).

The experience of "peace and quiet"—that is symbolized by the mouth of Christ at which the kiss of peace is given (according to the way it was done in some ancient rites of the Mass, such as the Dominican)[142]—is the fruit of this union. The Lord says: "These [souls] receive a fruit of the quiet of the mind, a union made through sentiment in my sweet divine nature, where they taste the milk" that gives an infinite sweetness to the virtues (c. 96). Peaces ensues in the soul after the "great war she waged because of her faults" (c. 26), peace acquired by the merit of the bitterness tasted by Jesus for us when he was on the cross and drank vinegar and gall (see letter 309). This peace and quiet does not signify inertia but rather that "in this third state the soul finds peace in such a way that there is no one who can disturb the soul because it has lost and drowned its will," and therefore it puts into practice the virtues to the benefit of the neighbor and so it is active without suffering or neglect of anyone or anything (c. 76)

Third, perfect union is a *union of the will* with God, that is to say of the affection of love, and consists in a perfect conformity of one's will and desire with God that is attained when one is completely free from sensitive self-will (ibid.) which opposes it and is filled with God and his love (see c. 45), so that God says of such a soul: "It is another me made so through the union of love"

(c. 96; letter 215). This is not a pure charismatic gift but the fruit of a charity that has been illumined, matured, and reinforced in the midst of problems, moral and corporal, which the soul has borne or even lovingly embraced for the honor of God and the salvation of souls. With this constant treatment, i.e., increasing conformity to the divine will, the sensitive appetite and self-will can no longer resist and, like an article of clothing that is too tight or an over-inflated balloon, it bursts and dies (see c. 76). Then the soul loves without reserve that which God loves and hates that which God hates, choosing always to serve God in his way and not ours; it sees the divine will in everything that happens or is imposed on it, and accepts it with love because "no matter where it is, it thinks of nothing else but to conform itself to that [divine] will" (c. 77).

There is another conformity with Christ crucified that is said to be "blessed and sorrowful:"[143] the most perfect are also sorrowful because of the "crucifying sorrow" that they bear at the offence done to God and the harm done to one's neighbor (verified by the saying, "The one who increases in love increases in sorrow"). They are blessed because the delight of charity cannot be taken from them (see cc. 78, 89). Love becomes a torment and the torment becomes joy because the sufferings that we experience are not "afflicting" but "fattening" (c. 78; see letter 119).

Perfect union is stable and secure, realized in free-will that is stabilized in God: "And yet they are so firm and stable in their will and in their going along the way of truth and not slackening their pace, faithfully serving their neighbor" without being offended or discouraged by any injury or ingratitude, lamenting only for what offends God and for the spiritual harm done by the one who insults God and neighbor (see c.77). With regard to the sensitive part of perfect union, however, the soul must not trust too much in itself because no one ever becomes completely insensitive to injuries and offences; it is only that "the sentiments seem to be sleeping." And now and again God permits, like a "pleasant deceit" meant to keep us humble, that one is woken up by "a tiny thing" that causes such resentment that will later appear to us as disproportionate and strange, so as to warn the soul to always be vigilant and ready to castigate sentiment so that it may return to sleep again (see c. 145).

The Sweet Signs

How can we know that the soul has attained to perfect love? By the virtues that shine now much more in the soul: "The precious stones of the virtues shining" (c. 146). The virtues are the "sweet signs" of recognition (c. 77) and are principally three: *patience, fortitude,* and *perseverance,* the latter to be understood less in the negative sense of being endured than in the positive sense of giving and offering to the neighbor charity in all his trials (see letter 357).[144]

Patience is "singularly above every sign" (c. 77), that is to say that it is the most conspicuous. We already know that it is, par excellence, "a demonstrative sign that shows that the soul loves perfectly and is without any self-regard. Because if the soul loves me or the neighbor for its own gain, it would be impatient and would slacken its pace" (c. 76). Indirectly a tribulation, when there is patience, becomes a "demonstrative sign that shows the [soul's] perfect charity," in other words it is the occasion that makes the soul patient; impatience is its opposite (c. 145; see c. 95). This is why patience is said to be a "queen that takes dominion and rules over all the virtues, because it is the marrow of charity" (c. 77); in fact, it proves if the virtues are alive and perfect, founded on the love of God or not (see c. 95).

Fortitude, which seems to be the fruit most apparent in the Pentecost mystery, makes us speak the truth without fear of suffering or death and fulfills the works of charity without being subject to the sensitive passions due to a participation in the divine power (see c. 74) and without turning "the head to look back at the plow" (c. 77), in other words without yielding to flattery, threats, or our own complacence.[145]

Perseverance is necessary to arrive at the end of every undertaking, whether good or bad (see c. 52), and therefore must accompany the other two virtues so that fortitude does not abandon the field of battle, and so that, in the end, patience "returns home with the victory" and receives from the Father "the crown of glory" (c. 77).

We need to add to these signs the almost heavenly harmony of the sentiments and of the soul's faculties as well as of all the saints and most perfect souls and their good works, a harmony similar to that of musical instruments which is so enchanting as to become a hook to catch sinners and bring them back to the life of grace (see c. 147).

Diverse and Admirable Gifts[146]

Often added in the unitive state (like the "gratiae gratis datae" [graces freely given] of the theologians) are "new and diverse gifts and admirable elevations [=illuminations] of the mind…with a knowledge of the truth [=enlightenment of faith] that although being mortal, one seems almost immortal" (c. 89). These are like the consolations of the first and second stairs, that is, they come freely given and not as ends in themselves but as means to increase charity. In fact, even at this stage one continues to progress, "because the soul is never so perfect in this life that it cannot grow to a greater perfection, that is, to a perfection of love," though it cannot climb to another stair being that this is the last one (c. 89). However, like all consolations, we must not be attached to these gifts, rather "the humble soul must always scorn them," taking no account of them but being happy with the fruit of internal virtues (c. 89).

Let us give some examples. Besides the elevations of the mind and illustrations of the truth that characterize the union of the mind, such as knowing how even sinners give glory to God (see c. 80), Catherine cites here the *"spirit of prophecy* to know future things" (c. 89). Catherine also alludes to the *stigmata*, considered as a refraction of the grace of Christ;[147] the marks seem to be like the wounds received in persecutions endured out of love for Christ and the good of souls. They are splendid testimonies of virtue because they denote how far love has brought these souls to disregard themselves, and therefore "the crucified love they have shines in the body" (c. 78), such as the luminous testimony of the stigmata imprinted on Catherine's flesh.[148]

The phenomena of *levitation* and *ecstasies* are described many times as the effects of union (see c. 79; letter 263) or transitory union: "Often, therefore, the body is lifted up from the earth because of the perfect union that the soul has with me, almost as if the heavy body had become light." And here is the reason: "It is not because the heaviness has been removed from the body, but because the soul's union with me is more perfect than the soul's union with the body" (c. 79; see letter 309). Then "it is as if the body is immobile, completely swept away by the soul's affection, meanwhile...it would no longer be possible to live if not that my goodness had not surrounded it with strength" (c. 79). At this point Catherine recalls her personal experiences—spoken in an impersonal form: "as you will recall having heard about some creature" (ibid.)—which she herself describes in another place.[149] The human body cannot bear for long this rapture or ecstatic union (see cc. 79, 94) and so it is interrupted by God—and sometimes also from the voice of one's religious superior (see c. 165)—and the soul is called back to the corporal bond that seemed suspended: "And for this reason I take away [ecstatic] union for some time, making the soul return to the vessel of its body; in other words, so that the body's sentiment, which was completely alienated from [the preponderance of] the soul's affection, returns." (c. 79).

Abstraction from the senses and *spiritual intoxication* are other "admirable signs" mentioned by Catherine. She often mentions these phenomena in a clear mystical sense in regard to the union of charity. Eternal love produces these acts through an infusion of charity: "And the Holy Spirit does this when it comes into the soul" (letter 30), dissolving in love the hardness of the heart. First of all "the vessel of its body loses every sentiment" (letter 263), in other words it loses contact with awareness of the "I" through the invasion of another "I": "that seeing it does not see, hearing it does not hear, speaking yet it does not speak, going yet it does not go, touching yet it does not touch. All the body's sentiments seem to be tied up and to have lost their power because affection has lost itself and is united with God" (letter 263).[150]

The analogy of being drunk on wine is effective insofar as its details are emphasized. It is not new; Catherine is very familiar with it as it is found in earlier patristic and mystical literature. It is when one is completely invaded by wine to the point that in the drunkard "nothing else is found but the feeling of wine; all the sentiments are immersed in the wine" (letter 25); "and when he has drunken well he throws up over the heads of his brothers" (letter 208); "when he is good and full [=completely drunk], he falls asleep; and when asleep, he feels neither prosperity nor adversity" (letter 75). These analogies have a clear application to the spiritual state in which all the powers of the soul are together "immersed and drowned" in God (c. 79) and the soul "no longer sees itself for itself, but itself for God, and we see God for God, and the neighbor for God" (letter 208), and it can do nothing less than pour forth its fullness on others (ibid.) and is neither moved by adverse or favorable things because it is full of fire and beatitude, stable and firm (see c. 78).

The *unitive tears* and *tears of fire*, proper to the third stair, are tears of sweetness through the union with God (the fifth state of tears) as well as tears of compassionate and active affection toward sinners because they have offended God and have inflicted harm on themselves: "weeping with those who weep and rejoicing with those who rejoice" (c. 89). They are perfect "unitive tears," showing that they come from an ardent soul from which the devil flees "like the fly from the boiling pot" (c. 90).

There is a kind of weeping that does not moisten the eye: they are the famous "tears of fire" denoting those who have not been able to have the gift of tears (see c. 91). These tears represent love and the desire of suffering, united together so as to make the heart burn for the Lord and for souls. The Holy Spirit, who is this same love, weeps in these souls which are "full of the fire of divine charity" (c. 91), and make a joyful torment in souls resigned to accept the dryness of the eyes (ibid.).

At the Gate of Heaven: Fourth State

The soul has arrived at such "perfect union...that, although being in a mortal body, tastes the reward of the immortals" (c. 145). After the stair of Christ's mouth there is no other stair. It is true that the perfect can always grow in perfection, "but not to another state"—as the Lord says—"because you have arrived at the last one" (c. 89). It is also true that earthly union, while perfect in grace, is imperfect compared to that of eternal life (see c. 96).

Perfect union is an anticipation of heaven, like a pledge of eternal life, which one can have here on earth in different ways. The virtues that come to us from heaven and make us similar to the angels are already a first reward in themselves and give us an anticipation of heavenly joys, just as vice and the sinner are an anticipation of eternal damnation (see c. 46). As the torments and illusions of sin are "the devil's cross" and give the "pledge of hell" because they are without hope of true and eternal happiness, so the joys and above all the hopes contained in all the virtues anticipate the enjoyment of the eternal reward so that even "in this same life the just have a better situation than sinners" (cc. 47-48).

The soul's victory over its enemies in this life is also a prelude to the final victory and a sign that God is in us. More predominant than any other sign is the "quiet of the soul" at peace with God, secure in its friendship and sure of going on the way to heaven (see c. 28). There is the happiness of knowing that all suffering lovingly accepted cooperates in the fulfillment of the divine desire to save us and is "one of the most extraordinary signs" (letter 354) to be found on the way of truth. The fact of having "holy desire" for one's sanctification is to have already taken food with the angels, which is angelic food (see letters 26, 353).[151]

The soul that has in itself more of that of which is heavenly is closer to the gate of heaven, almost like a down payment of the riches that that the soul will receive above; in fact, "the pledge [of perfect union] is a beginning down payment given to man by which he waits to receive full payment" (c. 101). This pledge or down payment is found, first of all, in the stability of that union of grace and sentiment, the fire of charity which neither sorrow nor suffering can take way and with a delight that can not be lost, that makes the soul to be already in someway blessed in this life (see c. 78). Those who have killed their self-will, against whom they have waged war, find in the mouth (third stair) enduring peace and quiet (see c. 76), "tasting eternal life, deprived of the hell of self-will, which was a pledge of hell to the man who lives according to the sensitive will" (c. 85). Their souls are positioned in union with God's will, which is an anticipation of heaven: "this is that most excellent state that, being also mortal, tastes bliss with the immortals" (ibid.). The state of ecstasy and spiritual intoxication, which we have already described in reference to this union, is a sign and pledge of beatitude: "Often so much union comes that one hardly knows if he is in the body or outside of it"— reminiscent of 2 Cor 12:2-3—"and one tastes the pledge of eternal life because of the union that it has made in me, and because the will is dead in the soul itself" (c.85).[152]

Can one have the beatific vision in this life? Can the most perfect attain it here below? It is necessary to understand the differences. "Do you know what the most extraordinary good is that the blessed [in heaven] have?"—asks Eternal Truth; and he answers —"It is to have their will full of what they desire. They desire me, and desiring me they have me and taste me" (c. 45). In this life, souls can have this only in part, but not directly; only in heaven is the soul's desire fully satisfied, "because desiring to see me, it sees me; in this vision is your beatitude" (ibid.) If put in terms of the beatific vision, the question has no other solution. It is clear that for Catherine one can have this vision only when "the soul has left the weight of the body" (c. 45). She speaks of "seeing me [=God] in the divine essence," and this is not on earth but in heaven, where "the saints, separated from the body, taste" true perfection (c. 83). Therefore, like Paul, those "who had arrived to the third and fourth state of perfect union which are in me, [are] crying with him and wanting to be freed and separated from the body" (ibid.).

The case of Paul who was caught up to the third heaven is both an exception and an example. An exception because, although the soul not being separated from the body, he was raised "to the height of the Trinity" (c. 83), being now able "to taste it…without the heaviness of the body," that is "through the sentiment of union but not through separation" (c. 83), although this was not a "vision of essence" (at least Catherine never says it), "face to face" which is the proper "vision of the immortal blessed" souls (c. 79). Paul's experience is an example, because the desire of "being freed and separated from the body" is attained in the complete perfection of seeing God in his essence and of tasting him without the impediment of the "bulk of the body" (c. 83). This way of being "impatient in living" is the soul's last "crucifying desire" that, united to sadness for the human fragility of sinners, makes the soul—"that dies but cannot die"—feel that this life is almost unbearable, even if one is conformed to the divine will (c. 84).

There remains the reality of the union attained on the last stair, union that brings knowledge and charity by the light of faith to the highest summit (see c. 45) and thus the desire of the soul to possess God with the entire human capacity in its earthly condition is fulfilled, to the maximum allowed in this life (ibid). Here we have, in fact, the union in God of the three powers that, by now free from all interference, are filled only with God, as we have seen (letter 263). There is also a seeing and tasting God "in the affection of charity," that even if it has to be called "darkness if compared with what is seen by the soul separated from the body" (c. 79), is, however, the nearest point to the gate of heaven toward which the union of union, ecstatic rapture, frequently makes small openings in the gate. "This is a seeing through infused grace that I give to the soul that truly loves and serves me" (c. 84).

Conclusion

It was worth the effort investigating the point to which Catherine pushed her research and exposition, to this summit of the bridge, so as to spur souls desirous of advancing securely to their goal. At this point even the "desire for death" (c. 84) becomes sweet, as Catherine has shown, because it is a serene, confident and active waiting for light eternal. It would be useful here to report the judgment of Pierre Pourrat, a noted scholar of Christian spirituality, who wrote: "This presentation of the transforming mystical union is one of the best that has been given."[153]

We conclude with the words of Eternal Truth: "O dearest daughter, enamored with this sweet and excellent state" (c. 100).

ENDNOTES

[1] The year is historically certain, but the traditional date of March 25 is not (D'Urso). See the Selected Bibliography at the end for a list of the primary sources of Catherine's life and contemporary biographies based on them.

[2] For more on the *Mantelatte* ("mantled ones") see Raymond of Capua, *The Life of Catherine of Siena,* trans. by Conleth Kearns, OP (Wilmington, DE: Michael Glazier, 1980; reprinted 1994 by Dominicana Publications, 487 Michigan Avenue N.E., Washington, DC 20017-1585), §§ 77-79, pp. 70-72 and *Dominican Penitential Women,* ed., trans. and intro. by Maiju Lehmijoki-Gardner. The Classics of Western Spirituality (New York: Paulist Press, 2005).

[3] Raymond of Capua, *The Life of Catherine of Siena,* trans. Kearns, §59, p. 55. (Kearn's translation differs slightly: "one continuous marvel.") Raymond's work is traditionally referred to as the *Legenda major.* Raymond's actual name was Raimondo delle Vigne (c. 1330–1399). He was Master of the Order of Preachers from 1380–99 and was beatified in 1899. In 1374 he was appointed by the then Master of the Order, Elias of Toulouse, as Catherine's confessor. For a biographical outline of Raymond, see Conleth Kearns' introduction in *The Life of Catherine of Siena,* xiii-liii.

[4] This incident of drinking the bath water has made many a would-be contemporary devotee of Catherine lose interest in her. Catherine's goal was to manifest her love of God, which knew no bounds, in her love of neighbor. Like many medievals, she desired to attain a level of self-conquest under the inspiration of grace. Molly Morrison, in "Strange Miracles: A Study of the Peculiar Happenings of St. Maria Maddelena de' Pazzi," *Logos* 8:1 (Winter 2005), pages 129-144, cites several examples of other medieval saints who went considerably further than Catherine.

[5] The question of the reality of the stigmata—although the historical fact was without doubt—was protracted at length in the Church, with various twists and turns, until Pope Benedict XIII authorized the celebration in the Dominican Order of the liturgical feast commemorating it. (D'Urso). William R. Bonniwell, OP, in *A History of the Dominican Liturgy* (New York: Wagner, 1944), pp. 249-251, 334, traces the centuries-old controversy between the partisans of St. Francis of Assisi and those of St. Catherine regarding the legitimacy of the latter's stigmata over which "the most disgraceful scenes of violence took place." The matter was resolved in 1727 by Dominican Pope Benedict XIII who granted permission to celebrate in the Dominican order the feast of the Stigmata of St. Catherine of Siena "with the rite of *duplex*" on April 1. It is no longer observed.

[6] In this work we will use the numbering system for the letters of Niccolò Tommaseo, which is more or less standard today. The translations of the letters, *Dialogue,* prayers, are my own. The entire Catherinian corpus has been translated into English by Suzanne Noffke, OP (see Selected Bibliography at the end of this work), with an index to all the letters according to the Tommaseo system at the end of vol. IV. Prior to Noffke, Vida Scudder translated eighty letters which were published in her *Saint*

Catherine of Siena as Seen in Her Letters (New York: Dutton, 1927), available online, and Kenelm Foster, OP, translated a small collection in *I, Catherine: Selected Writings of Catherine of Siena* (London: Collins, 1980). Foster's introduction to the work contains a superb summary of Catherine's spiritual thought. See www.drawnbylove.com.

[7] The Dominican order "is known to have been established, from the beginning, for preaching and the salvation of souls, especially." Prologue to the Primitive Constitutions, quoted in "The Fundamental Constitution," *The Book of Constitutions and Ordinations of the Brothers of the Order of Preachers* (Dominican Publications: Dublin, 2001), 25.

[8] Johannes Jorgensen, *Saint Catherine of Siena*, trans. Ingeborg Lund (London: Longman, 1938), p. 94.

[9] "[W]ith those prayers, tears and sweat I will wash the face of my spouse, the holy Church" (c. 86). See letter 371.

[10] See "Frères Prêcheurs" in *Dictionnaire de spiritualité ascétique et mystique,* vol. 5 (Paris: Beauchesne, cols. 1422-1524. (D'Urso). Internet: www.domcentral.org/study/ashley/ds00intr.htm

[11] It was at Pisa in 1375 that she received the stigmata. (D'Urso).

[12] "Ultime Parole" in Caterina da Siena, *Le lettere di Santa Caterina da Siena,* con note di Niccolò Tommaseo, a cura di Piero Misciattelli, vol. VI (Firenze: Giunti, 1940), p. 173. (D'Urso).

[13] John Paul II proclaimed St. Bridget of Sweden, St. Catherine of Siena, and St. Teresa Benedicta of the Cross (Edith Stein) co-patronesses of Europe on October 1, 1999.

[14] Anonymous, "On Consummated Perfection. A Brief Dialogue by St. Catherine of Siena," in Augusta Theodosia Drane, *The History of St. Catherine of Siena and Her Companions,* 3rd edition, vol. II (London: Longmans, 1899), pp. 345-355. Although it is not authentic, the document is imbued with Catherine's principles and themes, and could be regarded as a condensation of her teaching. At an earlier time some considered it as having been written by her.

[15] Robert Fawtier, *Saint Catherine de Sienne. Essai de critique des sources,* 2 vols., (Paris: DeBoccard, 1930).

[16] Eugenio Dupré-Theseider, "Sono autentiche le Lettere di Santa Caterina?" in *Vita Cristiana* XII, 1940, p. 239. (D'Urso).

[17] As done by Pagnone, *Fiori di eloquenza e di virtù*; re-edited by Cordovani as *Brevario di perfezione* and, lastly, with the title *Teologia dell'amore,* Rome, 1962 and 1968. (D'Urso).

[18] Raymond of Capua, *The Life of Catherine of Siena,* § 332, pp. 309-310, and §§ 342-343, pp. 317-318.

[19] The manuscripts are Senese T. II, 9, dictated to Maconi; Casanatense 292, to Canigiani. (D'Urso). See also Giuliana Cavallini, introduzione, Caterina da Siena, *Il dialogo* (Siena: Cantagalli, 1995), pp. xi-xlvii.

[20] *Memorie,* ed. by G. Milanesi. (D'Urso).

[21] The better edition of the Latin text is in *Acta Sanctorum,* April, III. (D'Urso). Caffarini's *Legenda minor* has yet to be translated in English. "The testimony of this earliest confessor [Tommaso della Fonte or "Caffarini"] of St. Catherine fills so large a place in Raymond's narrative that a summary account of the part he played seems desirable. He was called Father Thomas della Fonte. He was a younger brother of a son-in-law of Catherine's father, Giacomo Benincasa, in whose house he was 'brought up from childhood.' Older than Catherine, Thomas became a Dominican about the year 1356, while she was still a child of 9 or 10 years of age. Even before she took the habit of the Sisters of Penance he had become her first confessor, and thereafter remained her chief spiritual guide and counselor until, in 1374, he gave place to Raymond. To Raymond he handed over the copious notes which he had taken regarding Catherine's spiritual experiences and way of life over the 12 preceding years. He remained her faithful helper and disciple until her death in 1380, and an attached friend and frequent fellow-worker of Raymond until his own death in 1390. From his written records and from his *viva voce* testimony Raymond quotes repeatedly to describe and authenticate events of Catherine's life in the period previous to his own acquaintance with her. Unfortunately, as far as is known, the invaluable notebooks of Thomas della Fonte have not survived." Kearns, Raymond of Capua, *The Life of Catherine of Siena,* note on p. 33.

[22] Angel Morta, introducción in *Obras de Santa Catalina de Siena : El dialogo,* tr. Angel Morta (Madrid: B.A.C., 1955), p. 118. (D'Urso).

[23] Cornelius a Lapide, *Comm. in proph. Minor, in Zach.,* c. IX. (D'Urso).

[24] Niccolò Tommaseo, *Le lettere di S. Caterina da Siena,* vol. I (Firenze: Barbera, 1860). (D'Urso).

[25] Gino Capponi, *Storia della Republica Fiorentina* (Firenze, 1876). (D'Urso)..

[26] Giovanni Papini, *Storia della letteratura italiana,* vol. I (Firenze: Vallecchi), p. 432. (D'Urso).

[27] Jolanda DeBlasi, *Le scrittrici Italiane dalle origine al 1800* (Firenze, 1930), pp. 32 and 49. (D'Urso). For a more recent appraisal see Jane Tylus, *Reclaiming Catherine of Siena: Literacy, Literature, and the Signs of Others* (Chicago: University of Chicago Press, 2009) in which the author argues that Catherine should be put along side literary giants such as Dante and Petrarch.

[28] Pierre Pourrat, *Christian Spirituality*, vol. III (Westminister, MD: Newman Press, 1953), p. 250. First published in French in 1927 as *La spiritualité Chrétienne*.

[29] See Morta, introducción in *Obras de Santa Catalina de Siena : El dialogo*, p. 4. (D'Urso).

[30] Evelyn Underhill, *Mysticism. A study in the nature and development of man's spiritual consciousness* (New York: Dutton, 1930), p. 467. Eugenio Dupré-Theseider, who published in 1940 the first critical edition of eighty-eight of Catherine's letters, was a Waldensian.

[31] "May I know myself and know You." Augustine of Hippo, *Soliloquies*, Bk. II, i, 1.

[32] A(ntoine) Lemonnyer, OP, *Notre vie spirituelle à l'école de Sainte Catherine de Sienne* (Paris: Cerf, 1934), indice. (D'Urso).

[33] References to the *Dialogue* are to chapters; e.g., c. 43 means chapter 43 of the *Dialogue*. All translations are based on the text: Caterina da Siena, *Il dialogo della divina provvidenza di S. Caterina da Siena*, ed. Giuliana Cavallini, 2nd ed. (Siena: Cantagalli, 1995).

[34] Because authentic visions and revelations are not dependent on us, do not happen when we want them, and could be illusions of the devil. (D'Urso).

[35] We cannot always do corporal penances because of our health; often they kill the body but not the will. (D'Urso).

[36] See *Dialogue*, c. 119 and passim (D'Urso). Raymond of Capua, *The Life of Catherine of Siena*, trans. Kearns, §92, p. 85.

[37] "But Moses said to God, 'If I come to the Israelites and say to them, 'The God of your ancestors has sent me to you,' and they ask me, 'What is his name?' what shall I say to them?' God said to Moses, 'I AM WHO I AM.'" Exodus 3:13-14. Biblical quotations are taken from the New Revised Standard Bible unless otherwise noted.

[38] See Jn 8:34. (D'Urso).

[39] See letter 221 for a famous episode with regard to God in the will of one who is tempted. (D'Urso).

[40] "By our first parents' sin, the devil has acquired a certain domination over man, *even though man remains free.*" *Catechism of the Catholic Church*, §407. Henceforth abbreviated *CCC.* Emphasis mine. The inviolability of the will refers to the will's power to determine itself and to act of itself, without compulsion from within or coercion from without.

[41] Here Catherine reflects received spiritual wisdom: it is imprudent to enter into conversation with the devil as it exposes one to the danger of succumbing. See Jordan Aumann, *Spiritual Theology* (London: Sheed and Ward, 1980), p. 158.

[42] "We love God and hate ourselves—not the self that is [God's] creation, but the self we see rebelling against our Creator" (letter 101). Self-hatred for Catherine does not mean hating everything about oneself but only that which is sinful, i.e. "rebels" against God. When seen as a whole, her theological anthropology is exceptionally positive: e.g., the human person is made in the divine image and likeness, is "beautiful" and is called to divinization. (see c.1).

[43] Catherine is certainly not opposed to loving oneself so long as it is done in and for God and not apart from him. To love ourselves apart from him is "perverse self-love." We are obliged to love ourselves in the correct way, because we are our own "chief neighbor" (c. 6).

[44] "Let the little children come to me, and do not stop them; for it is to such as these that the kingdom of heaven belongs" Mt 19:14.

[45] "Negative" here means a withdrawal, removal, a drawing back or taking away

[46] That is, meriting an eternal prize. (D'Urso).

[47] Letter 345 is a very beautiful text, an eloquent analysis which should be read in its entirety. (D'Urso).

[48] The text of letter 38 is very beautiful and is a prelude to chapter 8 of *Lumen gentium.* (D'Urso).

[49] See also Chapter Four.

[50] We will see this when we examine the second stair in Chapter Six. (D'Urso).

[51] See Chapters Five –Seven.

[52] Catherine portrays conscience as a teacher with authority who speaks from a professorial chair or *sedia.*

[53] See the reasons for this in letters 340 and 213. (D'Urso).

[54] Blaise Pascal, *Pascal's Pensées* (New York: Dutton, 1958), no. 526, p. 169.

[55] Raymond of Capua, *The Life of Catherine of Siena*, trans. Kearns, § 49, p. 47.

[56] The Italian word for soul is *anima*, which belongs to the feminine grammatical gender. Some English translators of Catherine's works have used feminine pronouns in reference to the soul, e.g., "She [=the soul] always wants to love something." While this is certainly not incorrect, it can be distracting for English readers who are accustomed to thinking of the soul as neuter. For this reason, I have used neuter pronouns when referring to the soul.

[57] Prayer 17 in Noffke's edition of St. Catherine's prayers is a translation of prayer X in Cavalini's Italian edition of the prayers. See Catherine of Siena, *The Prayers of Catherine of Siena*, ed., trans., notes by Suzanne Noffke, OP, 2nd edition (San Jose, CA: Authors Choice Press, 2001); Caterina da Siena, *Le orazioni di S. Caterina da Siena*, a cura di Giuliana Cavallini (Roma: Edizioni Cateriniane, 1978). Noffke's translation is based on Cavallini's edition.

[58] A Thomistic thought. (D'Urso).

[59] Catherine stresses this theme incessantly in all her writings: "And that which he gave or permitted in our lives he gave only for this purpose: that [in heaven] we may participate in his supreme and eternal beauty" (letter 122; see letter 181, etc.; c. 135). (D'Urso).

[60] St. Paul, by exception, had the experience here on earth. (D'Urso). See 2 Cor 12:1-5.

[61] As St. Thomas Aquinas says in *Summa theologiae* I, 93, 7-8. (D'Urso). For an English translation, see Thomas Aquinas, *Summa theologica*, trans. Fathers of the English Province, 3 vols. (New York: Benziger Brothers, 1947).

[62] *De Trinitate* XIV, 8 and 12. (D'Urso).

[63] On incarnation and knowledge, see prayer 17/X. (D'Urso).

[64] See Raymond of Capua, *The Life of Catherine of Siena*, §§ 163, 187, 188, 191. (D'Urso).

[65] Charisms are literally "gifts of grace."

[66] "[T]hat we might participate in him" alludes to 2 Pet 1:4, "Thus he has given us, through these things, his precious and very great promises, so that through them you may escape from the corruption that is in the world because of lust, and *may become participants of the divine nature.*" This text is often cited in reference to the doctrine of divinization (deification).

[67] Species: Appearances of bread and wine after the eucharistic consecration.

[68] "The Fathers of the Church distinguished *oikonomia* from *theologia*; the latter term refers to the mystery of the internal life of the Trinity. The economy of salvation, on the other hand, refers to God's activity in creating and governing the world, particularly with regard to his plan for the salvation of the world in the person and work of Jesus Christ, a plan which is being accomplished through his Body the Church, in its life and sacraments; hence, the 'sacramental economy'." "Economy of Salvation (Divine Economy)" in Glosssary, *CCC,* p. 876.

[69] According to Aristotle, there are four causes of nature: material, formal, efficient, and final. The efficient cause is the agent which brings something about. D'Urso says that prayer is a *co*efficient cause which brings life-giving energy (sanctifying grace) to the Christian.

[70] *Cattedra* is Catherine's spelling of *cathedra* (Latin, "chair", from Greek, καθέδρα, "seat"), the chair, sometimes throne-like, of a bishop or professor which is a symbol of their teaching authority

[71] The "rule" is an allusion to the religious rule of monks, friars, nuns, etc.; e.g., the Rule of St. Augustine, the Rule of St. Benedict, etc.

[72] "No one has greater love than this, to lay down one's life for one's friends" (Jn 15:13).

[73] Jesus' last words on the cross, "I thirst," have been interpreted traditionally as signifying his intense desire for the salvation of souls.

[74] We have already seen this when we were speaking previously of the blood (see letters 9, 13, etc.). (D'Urso).

[75] Catherine's often-used way of describing the Pope.

[76] "Evangelical counsels" refer to the vows of poverty, chastity and obedience professed by consecrated persons such as monks, nuns, and friars.

[77] See c. 146 and prayer 19/XII. (D'Urso).

[78] Catherine attributes to "the doctors" of the Church the desire of Mary to make of herself a ladder so that she could put her Son on the cross if there was no other way to do so. The precise source is unknown. St. Bonaventure, in *Sententiae I,* dist. XLVIII (*Opere*, I, p. 861), says something similar: "In no way can it be doubted that [Mary's] courageous soul and most constant mind was willing even to give up her own Son for the salvation of the human race." See *The Letters of Catherine of Siena,* trans. S. Noffke, vol. I (Temple, AZ: Arizona Center for Medieval and Renaissance Studies, 2000), p. 112, n. 10.

[79] "Then Elisha prayed: 'O Lord, please open his eyes that he may see.' So the Lord opened the eyes of the servant, and he saw; the mountain was full of horses and chariots of fire all around Elisha" (2 Kings 6:17)

[80] Some scholars, such as Hurtaud, have speculated that the unnamed young man who was sentenced to death in letter 273, one of Catherine's most remarkable letters, was one Niccolò di Tuldo whom she ministered to right up to moment of his execution, having been instrumental in his conversion.

[81] The words "in the temple of our soul" refer to the indwelling of the Trinity in the soul, known as the doctrine of the divine indwelling and which is alluded in several passages in the New Testament, e.g. "Jesus answered him, 'Those who love me will keep my word, and my Father will love them, and we will come to them and make our home with them'" (Jn 14:23). See also Jn 14:20, Jn 15:4, 1 Jn 3:24, 1 Jn 4:13, 1 Jn 4:16, etc.

[82] It's possible that Catherine may have gotten the image of the tree of charity from Rev. 22:2.

[83] On holy self-hatred, see Chapter One, notes 12-13, p. 27.

[84] See *Summa theologiae* I-II, 27, I. (D'Urso).

[85] The chief supernatural virtues are faith, hope and charity; the chief natural (human, moral) virtues are prudence, justice, temperance, and fortitude. The supernatural virtues are infused by God; the natural or human virtues are acquired by the human person.

[86] Affections "are sentiments that pertain to the will, desires, and feelings, i.e., the outgoing activites. In the spiritual life they are identified with those movements of the soul that reach out to God.... Affections are acts of the infused virtues of hope and charity." John A. Hardon, SJ, *Modern Catholic Dictionary* (Garden City, NY: Doubleday, 1980), p. 15.

[87] At least by omitting the contribution of authentic prayer and thereby forfeiting the invisible influence of grace. (D'Urso)

[88] Catherine was aware of the theological distinction between charity and love. *Charity* is "[t]he infused supernatural virtue by which a person loves God above all things for his own sake, and loves others for God's sake" whereas *love* is an acquired natural virtue which means to will good to someone or to please someone. Basically there are two kinds of love. The love of concupiscence, or self-interested love, means that another is loved for one's own sake as something useful or pleasant to the one who loves. The love of friendship means selfless love of another for that person's own sake, for his or her good, to please him or her; it is the love of benevolence." Hardon, *Modern Catholic Dictionary,* pp. 95 and 325. Aumann sheds further light on charity: "The love that is charity, therefore, springs from a source that far transcends

human love and enables us to participate even now in that divine good which is our All. Such a love, coming from God, who is Love, enables us to return to him in an ecstasy of self-forgetfulness and to embrace our fellow-man in that same love, without becoming possessive or possessed by any human love. Achieving this, we fulfill Christ's supreme mandate of charity: 'Love one another as I loved you.'" Jordan Aumann, OP, "Thomistic Evaluation of Love and Charity," *Angelicum* 55 (1978), p. 555.

[89] Perhaps the battle imagery is derived from Rom 7:23, "I see in my members another law at war with the law of my mind, making me captive to the law of sin that dwells in my members."

[90] "From its use, it seems that *pregare* expresses above all the act of asking (petitions, questions), while *orare* means rather a way of communicating with God by conversing with him." Giacinto D'Urso, "Nozione teologale dell'orazione secondo S. Caterina," *Caterina da Siena* XVI (gennaio-febbraio 1965), p. 31. The word *preghiera(e)* appears only once (letter 338) in the Catherinian corpus.

[91] Patristic and medieval spiritual writers grappled with the meaning of St. Paul's injunction to "pray unceasingly" (1 Thes 5:17).

[92] Domenico Cavalaca, *Frutti di lingua,* chapter one. (D'Urso). Cavalca (c. 1270-1342) was a Dominican in Pisa who wrote popular spiritual works in the vernacular that had a wide circulation. D'Urso, in *Il genio di Santa Caterina* (Roma: Edizioni Cateriniane, 1971), pp. 112–114, identifies passages in every chapter of *Lo specchio* which, he says, are echoed in Catherine's writings. For more on Cavalca, see Benedict M. Ashley, OP, "Dominic Cavalca and a Spirituality of the Word," internet; keywords: ashley cavalca.

[93] Domenico Cavalca, *Lo specchio della croce,* testo orignale e versione in italiano corrente, a cura di P. Tito Sante Centi, OP (Bologna: Edizioni Studio Demenicano, 1992), chapter two, pp. 32-33.

[94] Like many medieval spiritual writers, Catherine adopts St. Augustine's triad of memory, intellect and will for the soul's three "powers" or faculties.

[95] An allusion to the parable of the return of the unclean spirit in Mt 12:43-45 and Lk 11:24-26.

[96] The subject of tears is a traditional theme in the history of Christian spirituality. "A rich, unbroken tradition of the Christian East and West up to the recent past sees tears as a normal feature of the spiritual life. The gift is seen as purifying and perfecting loving union with God and neighbor under the action of the Holy Spirit. ... Absence of tears is seen as signifying resistance to grace, e.g., Peter's tears (Mk 14:72) and Judas's lack of tears (Mt 27:5)." M. Claire Adams, OSC, "Tears, Gift of" in *The New Dictionary of Catholic Spirituality,* ed. Michael Downey. A Michael Glazier Book (Collegeville, MN: Liturgical Press, 1993), p. 957.

[97] Compare with cc. 31-35; 44; 48; 121-132; 150; 161. (D'Urso).

[98] For more on the universal call and the *scaloni generali* and *particulari*, see my *Catherine of Siena. Spiritual development in her life and teaching* (New York: Paulist Press, 2008), pp. 153-161.

[99] For "evangelical counsels" see Chapter Three, note 76.

[100] "God is not a respecter of persons" (Acts 10:34).

[101] S. Augustinus, *Tract. 48 in Joannem.* (D'Urso). Augustine of Hippo, *Homilies on the Gospel According to St. John by S. Augustine, Bishop of Hippo*, vol. II (Oxford: Parker; London: Rivington, 1898), p. 638.

[102] Catherine's "Spiritual Testament" is the account of her last words as recorded in Raymond of Capua's *Legenda maior*, nos. 360-367. "The first and fundamental point she made was, that one who comes to the service of God, if he be truly intent on entering into union with God, must strip his heart of all sense-love—not merely love of any other person, but of any created thing whatever." Raymond of Capua, *The Life of Catherine of Siena*, trans. Kearns, §360, p. 334.

[103] The notion of the body's "perverse law" is taken from St. Paul: "So I find it to be a law that when I want to do what is good, evil lies close at hand. For I delight in the law of God in my inmost self, but I see in my members another law at war with the law of my mind, making me captive to the law of sin that dwells in my members" (Rom 7:21-23).

[104] By "sensitive will" Catherine means the will under the influence of the body's senses.

[105] Cavalca, *Lo specchio della croce*, a cura di Sante Centi, chapter two, p. 33.

[106] D'Urso doesn't specify where Catherine may have had contact with St. Gregory's commentary (or what that commentary was), but it is possible that it is found in Cavalca's vernacular *Vite dei santi padre*, which I have not seen.

[107] "Like a dog that returns to its vomit is a fool who reverts to his folly" (Prov 26:11).

[108] In the Catherinian corpus, *sentiments* are feelings.

[109] I have translated here the word *figli* as "sons" because it corresponds to the biblical son who is the heir as well as to the Son of God. However, the word can also mean "children" or "offspring" and therefore applies to both men and women.

[110] Liberal means to give freely and generously, not out of fear or expectation of reward. St. Thomas Aquinas treats the virtue of liberality in *Summa theologiae* II-II,

[111] D'Urso refers here to the ancient division of the spiritual journey into three stages or ways (purgative, illuminative, and unitive) or three ages (incipient, proficient, perfect). Only the words *purgative, unitive* and *perfect* appear in Catherine's writings.

[112] Jn 14:21. (D'Urso). "They who have my commandments and keep them are those who love me; and those who love me will be loved by my Father, and I will love them and reveal myself to them."

[113] "I do not call you servants any longer, because the servant does not know what the master is doing; but I have called you friends, because I have made known to you everything that I have heard from my Father" (Jn 15:15).

[114] Consolations are effects of the action of the Holy Spirit in the soul and may include the action of consoling, cheering or comforting. Catherine uses the word in referring to these enjoyable effects. The ancient hymn *Veni, Sancte Spiritus* contains descriptions of the Spirit's various effects.

[115] "For where two or three are gathered in my name, I am there among them" (Mt 18:20).

[116] An allusion to Jn 20:17: "Jesus saith to her: Do not touch me: for I am not yet ascended to my Father" (Douay-Rheims).

[117] "Since it belongs to the supernatural order, grace *escapes our experience* and cannot be known except by faith." *CCC*, § 2005.

[118] Attachments are "repeated and willed clinging to things less than God for their own sakes." Thomas Dubay, SM, *Fire Within. St. Teresa of Avila, St. John of the Cross, and the Gospel on Prayer* (San Francisco: Ignatius, 1989), p. p. 135.

[119] It has been suggested that Bl. Teresa of Calcutta persevered through a most extended period of aridity lasting many years. See *Mother Teresa: Come Be My Light. The private writings of the "Saint of Calcutta"* edited with commentary by Brian Kolodiejchuk (New York: Doubleday, 2007).

[120] Aridity is "the state of a soul devoid of sensible consolation, which makes it very difficult to pray. It may be caused by something physical, such as illness, or voluntary self-indulgence, or an act of God, who is leading a person through trial to contemplation." John A. Hardon, S.J., *Modern Catholic Dictionary* (Garden City, NY: Doubleday, 1980), p. 41. Dryness, dullness, flatness in the spiritual life.

[121] Some examples of extraordinary graces: visions, locutions, revelations, reading of hearts, stigmata, prophecy, levitation. Catherine, in *Dialogue* c. 89, counsels that extraordinary mystical phenomena should never be sought but rather shunned.

[122] That is, a given virtue is proven and strengthened when it is opposed by the corresponding vice, e.g., chastity is tested and strengthened when one overcomes carnal temptations.

[123] *Summa theologiae* II-II, q. 23, a.1 and 5. (D'Urso).

[124] "When it was evening on that day, the first day of the week, and the doors of the house where the disciples had met were locked for fear of the Jews, Jesus came and stood among them and said, 'Peace be with you'" (Jn 20:19).

[125] *Sermo* 61, 4 in *Canticum Canticorum*; *PL* 183, col. 1072. (D'Urso).

[126] Today in the Litany of the Sacred Heart we say: "fornax ardens caritatis" ("burning furnace of charity"). (D'Urso). The litany, a synthesis of other litanies dating back to the 17th century, was approved for public use by Leo XIII in 1899.

[127] In *Dialogue* cc. 74 and 78 Catherine presents the spiritual life as comprising four states (or stages) on the three stairs of the Bridge of Christ crucified, departing from the traditional threefold schema of purgative, illuminative, and unitive ways.

[128] Catherine's teaching on the universal call to holiness of all the baptised was affirmed most clearly at the Second Vatican Council (1962-65): "...all in the Church, whether they belong to the hierarchy or are cared for by it, are called to holiness, according to the apostle's saying: 'For this is the will of God, your sanctification'"(1 Thes 4:3; cf. Eph 1:4), *Lumen Gentium,* 39. Prior to the Council, Dominicans such as Juan González Arintero and Reginald Garrigou-Lagrange were instrumental in preparing the way for this new articulation of an old and somewhat overlooked truth. See Richard Peddicord, OP, *The Sacred Monster of Thomism: An introduction to the life and legacy of Reginald Garrigou-Lagrange, OP* (South Bend, Indiana: St. Augustine's Press, 2005).

[129] That is, for the salvation of souls.

[130] "He removes every branch in me that bears no fruit. Every branch that bears fruit he prunes to make it bear more fruit" (Jn 15:2).

[131] Passions are intense motions of a human appetite such as anger, sex, envy. They are desires which are out of control owing to fallen human nature.

[132] Meaning "every perfection is by means of the neighbor." (D'Urso).

[133] In *Dialogue,* c. 64, the Eternal Father tells Catherine, "Any love you have for me you owe me, so you love me not gratuitously but out of debt, while I love you gratuitously." In other words, we owe love to God for having created us and sustaining us in existence, whereas God needs nothing and therefore owes us nothing. His love for us is completely gratuitous.

[134] To be sanctified is to be divinized or deified, i.e., to participate in the divine nature. "Constituted in a state of holiness, man was destined to be fully 'divinized' by God in glory." *CCC,* § 398. See also § 1999.

[135] *Sermo* 3 and 4 in *Canticum Canticorum.* (D'Urso).

[136] Here again Catherine's teaching stays closes to the New Testament, particularly St. Paul: "So through God you are no longer a slave but a son, and if son then an heir" (Gal 4:7). See also Rm 8:15-16 and Lk 15:31. Theologians call this the doctrine of divine filial adoption. The son's "inheritance" corresponds to the doctrine of divinization or deification, when we "become partakers of the divine nature" (2 Peter 1:4).

[137] By "apostolic tendency" is meant the attraction to Christ's command to "make disciples of all the nations" (Mt 28:19). It is a matter of bringing people to the knowledge and love of Christ so that they might have eternal life.

[138] This is the third state, the first of two states which constitute the third stair. The third state is the state of "perfect union" (of the soul with God) and the fourth state is the state of "most perfect union."

[139] A reference to Jn 20: 19 where the disciples are huddled together in the Upper Room before Christ's resurrection.

[140] "[W]hether sacramental or virtual" refers to the actual reception of the Eucharistic species or its "virtual" reception by means of "spiritual communion." In the case of the latter, a person who is for some reason unable to receive the actual Sacrament expresses in prayer his or her desire to receive it spiritually.

[141] The "double cell of knowledge" refers to Catherine's image of a monastic cell within another cell as found in letters 49 and 94. The first cell represents knowledge of oneself, and the second one is knowledge of God and his goodness in us. For more, see my *Catherine of Siena. Spiritual development in her life and teaching*, pp. 121-124 or "Catherine of Siena's Teaching on Self Knowledge," *New Blackfriars* 88 (November 2007), pp. 637-648.

[142] The *Pax* or Kiss of Peace in the Eucharistic liturgy was originally an actual kiss but was later modified in all the rites. "In the West the traditional practice was for the person giving the Peace to place his hands on the shoulders of the recipient, who in turn placed his hands on the elbows of the giver, each bowing their heads towards each other." "Kiss of Peace" in *The Oxford Dictionary of the Christian Church* edited by F.L. Cross. Second edition (London: Oxford University Press, 1974), p. 785.

[143] The "viator" (wayfarer or pilgrim) and "comprehensor" (one who has reached the goal) spoken of by St. Thomas Aquinas in *Summa theologiae* III, 15, 10. (D'Urso)

105

[144] The expression *dolci segni* (sweet signs) appears in *Dialogue* c. 77 in reference to the characteristics of those on the third stair. The Italian word *dolce* could also be translated as gentle, pleasant, agreeable.

[145] "Jesus said to him, 'No one who puts a hand to the plow and looks back is fit for the kingdom of God'" (Lk 9:62).

[146] This is Catherine's way of describing extraordinary mystical phenomena.

[147] "The stigmata of Christ shines in them [who are] following his sweet doctrine" (letter 333). (D'Urso).

[148] See Raymond of Capua, *The Life of Catherine of Siena,* trans. Kearns, §195, p. 186. (D'Urso).

[149] See letters 381 to Urban VI and 373 to Raymond of Capua where Catherine says: "I saw my body as if it were someone else's." (D'Urso).

[150] Abstraction from the senses refers to the withdrawal of the external senses from the soul as might occur, for example, in ecstasy. St. Thomas Aquinas, in his treatment on the charism of prophecy in *Summa theologiae* II-II, q. 173, 3, distinguishes different types of abstraction from the senses.

[151] In letter 26 Catherine says that she desires to see her niece enjoying the food of angels which is, she explains, "God's desire in us" which draws our human desire to unite with it. Catherine, as with other mystics, sometimes speaks of union with God as a union of the divine and human will.

[152] 2 Cor 12:2-4, "I know a person in Christ who fourteen years ago was caught up to the third heaven—whether in the body or out of the body I do not know; God knows. And I know that this person was caught up into Paradise—whether in the body or out of the body I do not know; God knows. And he heard things that cannot be told, which a person may not utter."

[153] Pourrat, *Christian Spirituality*, vol. II, p. 209. (D'Urso).

SELECTED BIBLIOGRAPHY
Including Works Cited

AA.VV. "Frères Prêcheurs." *Dictionnaire de spiritualité ascétique et mystique.* Paris: Beauchesne, 1964. Vol. 5, cols. 1422-1524.

Adams, M. Claire, OSC. "Tears, Gift of." *The New Dictionary of Catholic Spirituality,* ed. Michael Downey. A Michael Glazier Book. Collegeville, MN: Liturgical Press, 1993.

Anonymous. "On Consummated Perfection. A Brief Dialogue by St. Catherine of Siena." In Augusta Theodosia Drane, *The History of St. Catherine of Siena and Her Compassions.* 3rd ed. London: Longmans, 1899. Vol. II, pp. 345-355.

Ashley, Benedict, OP. "Dominic Cavalca and a Spirituality of the Word." http://domcentral.org/dominic-cavalca-and-a-spirituality-of-the-word/.

Ashley, Benedict M., OP. "Guide to Saint Catherine's Dialogue." *Cross and Crown* 29 (September 1977): pp. 237–249.

Ashley, Benedict M., OP. "St. Catherine of Siena's Principles of Spiritual Direction." *Spirituality Today* 33:1 (March 1981): pp. 43–52.

Augustine of Hippo. *Expositions of the Psalms.* Trans. Maria Boulding, OSB. The Works of St. Augustine: A Translation for the 21st Century. Hyde Park, NY: New City Press, 2003.

Augustine of Hippo. *Homilies on the Gospel According to St. John by S. Augustine, Bishop of Hippo.* Oxford: Parker; London: Rivington, 1898.

Augustine of Hippo. *The Trinity.* Ed. John E. Rotelle. New York: New City Press, 1991.

Aumann, Jordan, OP. *Spiritual Theology.* London: Sheed and Ward, 1980. See: http://domcentral.org/spiritual-theology-1982/

Aumann, Jordan, OP. "Thomistic Evaluation of Love and Charity." *Angelicum* 55 (1978): pp. 534-556.

Bernard of Clairvaux. *The Works of Bernard of Clairvaux.* Vol. 2, *On the Song of Songs* I. Trans. Kilian Walsh; intro. M. Corneille Haflants. Spencer, MA: Cistercian Publications, 1993.

Bibliografia analitica di S. Caterina da Siena 1901–1950, 1961-1975, 1976-1985, 1986-1990, 1991-2000. 5 vols. Ed. Lina Zanni, Maria Carlotta Paterna. Roma: Centro Nazionale di Studi Cateriniani, 1971, 1985, 1989, 2000, 2003.

Bonaventure, Saint. *The Works of Bonaventure: Cardinal, Seraphic Doctor, and Saint.* Trans. José de Vinck. 5 vols. Paterson, NJ: St. Anthony Guild Press, 1960-1970.

Bonniwell, William R., OP. *A History of the Dominican Liturgy.* New York: Wagner, 1944.

Book of Constitutions and Ordinations of the Brothers of the Order of Preachers. Dublin: Dominican Publications, 2001.

Capponi, Gino. *Storia della Republica Fiorentina.* Firenze, 1876.

Catechism of the Catholic Church, 2nd edition. Città del Vaticano: Libreria

Editrice Vaticana, 1997.

Caterina da Siena. *Il dialogo della divina provvidenza di S. Caterina da Siena.* A cura di Giuliana Cavallini. Siena: Edizioni Cantagalli, 1995.

Caterina da Siena. *Le lettere di Santa Caterina da Siena.* Con note di Niccolò Tommaseo, a cura di Piero Misciattelli. 6 vols. Firenze: Giunti, 1940.

Caterina da Siena. *Le orazioni di S. Caterina da Siena.* A cura di Giuliana Cavallini. Roma: Edizioni Cateriniane, 1978.

Caterina da Siena. "Ultimate Parole." Caterina da Siena, *Le lettere di Santa Caterina da Siena,* con note di Niccolò Tommaseo, a cura di Piero Misciattelli. Firenze: Giunti, 1940: Vol. VI, pp. 173ff.

Catherine of Siena: *The Dialogue.* Trans. and intro. Suzanne Noffke, OP. Preface Giuliana Cavallini. The Classics of Western Spirituality. New York and Mahwah: Paulist Press, 1980.

Catherine of Siena. *I, Catherine: Selected Writings of Catherine of Siena.* Ed. and trans. Kenelm Foster, OP, and Mary John Ronayne, OP. St. James Place, London: Collins, 1980.

Catherine of Siena. *The Letters of Catherine of Siena.* Trans., intro., notes Suzanne Noffke. 4 vols. Medieval and Renaissance Texts and Studies. Temple: AZ: Arizona Center for Medieval and Renaissance Studies, 2000-2009.

Catherine of Siena. *The Prayers of Catherine of Siena.* Ed., trans., notes Suzanne Noffke, OP. 2nd edition. San Jose: Authors Choice Press, 2001.

Catherine of Siena. *Saint Catherine of Siena as Seen in Her Letters.* Trans., ed., notes Vida D. Scudder. London: Dent; New York: Dutton, 1927.

Cavalca, Domenico. *Lo specchio della croce.* Ed. Tito Sante Centi, OP. Bologna: Edizioni Studio Domenicano, 1992.

Cavallini, Giuliana. *Catherine of Siena.* Outstanding Christian Thinkers Series. London: Geoffrey Chapman, 1998.

Curtayne, Alice. *Saint Catherine of Siena.* London: Sheed and Ward, 1929.

DeBlasi, Jolanda. *Le scrittrici Italiane dalle origine al 1800.* Firenze, 1930.

Dominic, Sr. [Ann Walsh, OP.] "St. Catherine of Siena: Doctor of the Church." *Supplement* to *Doctrine and Life* 8 (1970): pp. 134–144.

Drane, Augusta Theodosia. *The History of St. Catherine of Siena and Her Companions.* 4th edition. 2 vols. London: Longman, Green and Co., 1915.

Dubay, Thomas, SM. *Fire Within. St. Teresa of Avila, St. John of the Cross, and the Gospel on Prayer.* San Francisco, CA: Ignatius Press, 1989.

Dupré Theseider, Eugenio. "Sono Autentiche le Lettere di Santa Caterina?" *Vita Cristiana* XII (1940): pp. 212-248.

D'Urso, Giacinto, OP. *Il genio di Santa Caterina.* Roma: Edizioni Cateriniane, 1971.

D'Urso, Giacinto, OP. "Nota Biografica." Santa Caterina da Siena. *L'estasi e la parola: Dialogo della divina provvidenza, lettere, orazioni.* Testi scelti a cura di Giacinto D'Urso. Fiesole: Nardini Editore, 1996. Pp. 43-35.

D'Urso, Giacinto, OP. "Nozione teologale dell'orazione secondo S. Caterina." *Caterina da Siena* XVI (gennaio-febbraio 1965): pp. 31-36 pp.

Fatula, Mary Ann, OP. *Catherine of Siena's Way.* The Way of the Christian Mystics Series. Wilmington, Delaware: Michael Glazier, 1987.

Fawtier, Robert. *Saint Catherine de Sienne. Essai de critique des sources,* 2 vols. Paris: DeBoccard, 1930.

Foster, Kenelm, OP. Introduction to *I, Catherine: Selected Writings of Catherine of Siena.* Ed. trans. Kenelm Foster, OP, and Mary John Ronayne, OP. St. James Place, London: Collins, 1980: pp.11–44.

Foster, Kenelm, OP. "The Spirit of St. Catherine of Siena." *Life of the Spirit* 15 (1961): pp. 433–446.

Foster, Kenelm, OP. "St. Catherine's Teaching on Christ." *Life of the Spirit* 16 (1962): pp. 310–323.

Gardner, Edmund G. *Saint Catherine of Siena. A study in the religion, literature, and history of the fourteenth century in Italy.* London: Dent; New York: Dutton, 1907.

Hardon, John A., SJ. *Modern Catholic Dictionary.* Garden City, NY: Doubleday, 1980.

John Paul II. Apostolic Letter *Amantissima Providentia. Acta Apostolicae Sedis* LXXII (April 1980): pp. 569–581. English translation: *L'Osservatore Romano,* Weekly Edition in English, June 23, 1980: pp. 7–8.

John Paul II. Apostolic Letter *Novo millennio ineunte. Acta Apostolicae Sedis* XCIII (3 mai 2001): pp. 266–309.

Jorgensen, Johannes. *Saint Catherine of Siena.* London: Longmans, 1938.

"Kiss of Peace." *The Oxford Dictionary of the Christian Church.* 2nd ed. Ed. F.L. Cross. London: Oxford University Press, 1974. Page 785.

Lapide, Cornelius a. *Commentary on the Minor Prophets: Zachariah* IX.

Lehmijoki-Gardner, Maiju, ed. *Dominican Penitent Women.* The Classics of Western Spirituality. New York: Paulist Press, 2005.

Lemonnyer, Antoine, OP. *Notre vie spirituelle à l'école de Sainte Catherine de Sienne* Paris: Cerf, 1934.

Levasti, Arrigo. *My Servant, Catherine.* Trans. Dorothy M. White. London: Blackfriars, 1954.

Luongo, F. Thomas. *The Saintly Politics of Catherine of Siena.* Ithaca: Cornell University Press, 2006.

McDermott, Thomas, OP. *Catherine of Siena. Spiritual development in her life and teaching.* New York: Paulist Press, 2008.

McDermott, Thomas, OP. "Drawn by Love. The Mysticism of Catherine of Siena." Website. www.drawnbylove.com

McGinn, Bernard. "Catherine of Siena: Apostle of the Blood of Christ." *Theology Digest* 48:4 (2001): pp. 329–342.

Milanesi, G. *Memorie.*

Morrison, Molly. "Strange Miracles: A Study of the Peculiar Happenings of

St. Maria Maddelena de' Pazzi." *Logos* 8:1 (Winter 2005): pp. 129-144.

Morta, Angel. Introducción in *Obras de Santa Catalina de Siena: El dialogo*. Trans. Angel Morta. Madrid: B.A.C., 1955.

Noffke, Suzanne, OP. "Catherine of Siena, Justly Doctor of the Church?" *Theology Today* 60 (2003): pp. 49–62.

Noffke, Suzanne, OP. *Catherine of Siena: Vision Through a Distant Eye*. A Michael Glazier Book. Collegeville, MN: The Liturgical Press, 1996.

O'Brien, Elmer, SJ. *Varieties of Mystic Experience*. New York: New American Library, 1964.

O'Driscoll, Mary, OP, ed. *Catherine of Siena: Passion for the Truth, Compassion for Humanity. Selected Spiritual Writings*. Hyde Park, NY: New City Press, 1993.

O'Driscoll, Mary, OP. "Catherine the Theologian." *Spirituality Today* 40 (Spring 1988): pp. 4–17.

O'Driscoll, Mary, OP. "St. Catherine of Siena: Life and Spirituality." *Angelicum* 57 (1980): pp. 305–323.

O'Driscoll, Mary, OP. "Women and the Dominican Tradition with Particular Reference to Catherine of Siena." *Angelicum* 81:2 (2004): pp. 445–457.

Pagnone, Alfonso M, ed. *Fiori di eloquenza e di virtù raccolti dalle Lettere di S. Caterina da Siena*. Torino : S. Giuseppe, 1872.

Papini, Giovanni. *Storia della letteratura Italiana*. Vol. 1. Firenze: Vallecchi, 1937.

Pascal, Blaise. *Pascal's Pensees*. New York: Dutton, 1958.

Paul VI. Apostolic Letter *Mirabilis in Ecclesia Deus*. (The Title of Doctor of the Universal Church is Conferred on Saint Catherine of Siena, October 4, 1970). *Acta Apostolicae Sedis* 63:9 (September 30, 1971): pp. 674–682.

Peddicord, Richard, OP. *The Sacred Monster of Thomism. An introduction to the life and legacy of Reginald Garrigou-Lagrange, OP*. South Bend, IN: St. Augustine's Press, 2005.

Pourrat, Pierre. *Christian Spirituality*. 4 vols. Westminister, MD: Newman Press, 1953.

Raymond of Capua. *The Life of Catherine of Siena* [Legenda Major]. Trans., intro., notes Conleth Kearns, OP. Wilmington, DE: Michael Glazier, 1980.

Teresa, Mother (Blessed Teresa of Calcutta). *Come Be My Light. The private writings of the "Saint of Calcutta."* Ed. with commentary Brian Kolodiejchuk, MC. New York: Doubleday, 2007.

Thomas Aquinas, Saint. *Summa Theologica*. Trans. Fathers of the English Dominican Province. 3 vols. New York: Benziger Brothers, 1947.

Tylus, Jane. *Reclaiming Catherine of Siena. Literacy, literature and the signs of others*. Chicago: University of Chicago Press, 2009.

Underhill, Evelyn. *Mysticism. A study in the nature and development of man's spiritual consciousness*. New York: Dutton, 1927.

www.ingramcontent.com/pod-product-compliance
Lightning Source LLC
LaVergne TN
LVHW022318080426
835509LV00036B/2583